1889 | 2014

DE

125 YEARS

DWIGHT-ENGLEWOOD SCHOOL

CELEBRATING OUR STORY

Englewood

DE

1889 | 2014

DE

125 YEARS

DWIGHT-ENGLEWOOD SCHOOL

CELEBRATING OUR STORY

The Donning Company Publishers
184 Business Park Drive, Suite 206
Virginia Beach, VA 23462

Steve Mull, General Manager
Barbara Buchanan, Office Manager
Heather L. Floyd, Editor
Brett Oliver, Graphic Designer
Kathy Adams, Imaging Artist
Susan Adams, Project Research Coordinator
Nathan Stufflebean, Marketing and Research Supervisor
Katie Gardner, Marketing Assistant

Mary Miller, Project Director

Library of Congress Cataloging-in-Publication Data

Dwight-Englewood School : celebrating our story / Karl Zimmerman, editor.
pages cm
ISBN 978-1-57864-897-9 (hardcover : alk. paper)
1. Dwight-Englewood School (Englewood, N.J.)--History. 2. Dwight-Englewood School (Englewood, N.J.)--History--Pictorial works. I. Zimmermann, Karl, 1943- editor.
LD7501.E52D85 2014
371.009749'21--dc23
2014011743

Printed in the United States of America at Walsworth Publishing Company

—TABLE OF CONTENTS—

FOREWORD

Dear Friends:

As we celebrate this year the 125th anniversary of Dwight-Englewood School, each of us has been provided an opportunity to reflect on the school's rich history; to recognize the accomplishments of our alumni, faculty, staff, families, and current students; and to clarify our vision going forward. Today's Dwight-Englewood—formed and enriched through a series of strategic mergers and thoughtful partnerships over the past years between Dwight School, the Englewood School for Boys, and the Bede School—represents not just a dynamic physical space but also a highly productive foundational experience for thousands of life-long learners. As such, the school has come to be a meaningful experience for everyone who has been a part of its history and who aims to shape its future.

Within the pages of this commemorative book we are excited to present the narratives of our richly diverse, amazingly talented, and wonderful community. We chose the theme of "Celebrating our Story" for our anniversary year to encourage everyone in our community to pause and reflect on the countless memories, vignettes, and testimonials typically shared by all those within our school, who when given the opportunity to talk about the school are proud and swift to do so. Special "D-E 125" events that took place this year, particularly those featuring our alumni, have brought to light the impact that Dwight-Englewood has had on our Englewood neighborhood, the New York City metropolitan area, and, indeed, the world. A consistent theme threaded throughout these narratives and events is the work of our dedicated faculty, which has held together the multifaceted fabric of each generation that has passed through our campus. Our teachers are engaged in the full life of our students, educating, supporting, and knowing them far beyond their academic experience. It is abundantly clear that our Core Values of respect, honesty, judgment, commitment, courage, and community are embraced by all who have a Dwight-Englewood story to share, if not a chapter or more.

Stories bring milestone events and society-benefiting acts and initiatives to life. Stories prompt us to consider again the lessons of our mentors. Stories inspire us to think about how we, too, can "make it better."

I invite you to enjoy our stories—stories that celebrate Dwight-Englewood School.

Warmly,
Dr. Rodney V. De Jarnett
Head of School

-ACKNOWLEDGMENTS-

Much like the Dwight-Englewood School itself, this book results from the generous collaboration of many. Especially notable among them are the former teachers and administrators who contributed chapters or timeline segments wholesale: Rebecca Blackwell Neely, Malcolm Duffy, and Joan Sommer. Some current faculty did the same: Steve Petkus, librarian and English teacher; Carole DeVito, chair of the history department; and John McCabe of the drama department. By virtue of their roles at D-E, others currently on staff did much of the heavy lifting that has made this book possible: Maria Sanchez Gardner '78, alumni director; Joni Hartsough, archivist; Liz Tausner, communications director; and Rodney De Jarnett, head of school. Summer interns Jeremy Chinman '12, Patrick Gardner, and Claudine Scrivanich helped out as well.

Others who provided background information include Robert Carson, former teacher and administrator; alumna Linda Reiter '78; Krish Pamani '14; and Sandra A. Latzer, librarian. For the school's centennial in 1989, a student committee, under the guidance of Ms. DeVito, created a slim but readable and fact-filled history, *The First Hundred Years*. Pictures and information from that book have proven invaluable in the creation of this one. Responding to a questionnaire constructed by Bill Bierce '67, many alumni shared photographs, memorabilia, and memories of their time at the schools. Bits and pieces of these recollections are found in this book, as well as in this year's issues of *D-E Today* and the 125th anniversary microsite (www.d-e.125.org).

Superintending this current book has been a wonderful opportunity for me to renew my acquaintance with the school at which I spent so many happy years, four as a student and thirteen as a teacher and administrator. All we alumni and former faculty can only be delighted by and proud of our school's growth and current robust state.

Karl Zimmermann '61
Editor

THE TIMELINE
A TAPESTRY RICH AND COLORFUL

As Dwight-Englewood celebrates the 125th anniversary of the oldest of its three heritage schools, our story is a complex tapestry, woven over a century and a quarter by countless hands. Nonetheless, in its final form—the Dwight-Englewood School we know today—this image made of many threads is strong, assured, and coherent, a collaborative work that is clear, colorful, and unambiguous.

The Dwight-Englewood story is actually many individual stories: narratives told, written, or remembered by teachers, students, school leaders, and heads of school and governing boards, all dedicated to making Dwight School, the Englewood School for Boys, the Bede School, and now the Dwight-Englewood School the best they could be.

This important anniversary is a perfect time to remember and honor the thousands of individuals who have played a part in the still-evolving, vibrant story of our school. It's a time to celebrate our past, learn from it, and take inspiration for the future. The following timeline chronicles the evolution and changes in program, physical plant, and leadership while highlighting some of the school's signal accomplishments.

1880s

1889: Dwight School was founded as a "Home and Day School" by Euphemia S. Creighton, who remained as co-principal and then principal until 1928, and Ellen W. Farrar, who was co-principal until 1920. They named it after the then-president of Yale College, Rev. Timothy Dwight, a close friend whose educational philosophy they respected. There had been private schools for girls in Englewood since 1859; Misses Creighton and Farrar, who had taught together in Rye, New York, bought the last of these, which had been run by a Miss Platt and Mrs. Peck. Dwight's first students, taught by a faculty of five, numbered fifty, including seven boarders. Several of the younger day students were boys.

Before Dwight School there was the Englewood Institute, founded by a Mrs. Peck and shown here circa 1884. Misses Creighton and Farrar purchased the school's equipment to found their own.

EUPHEMIA CREIGHTON

"Be sure and rule your work and do not let it rule you, even though you love it and must do it well. Do not let it cramp you, and rise above the routine. Keep your interest in the world at large. Enjoy life, enter into many of the interests.

Be a real whole-souled citizen." *From a letter to a graduate written by Euphemia Creighton.*

ELLEN FARRAR

"In closing she told the school that those who study there can take pride in the fact that their school was founded by a woman who was far in advance of her day in education, and whose philosophy of education has been carried along intact." *From an address given by Marion Howarth at a special chapel service to honor Miss Farrar.*

1890s

1891: In June, eight girls became Dwight's first graduates.

Dwight's Class of 1891, the first graduates.

1893: Dwight House was built as a residence for faculty and boarders, who came from as far away as Venezuela and India. Until this time Dwight had no permanent home. Dwight House later served as a dining room and then as a classroom building for Middle School students before Dwight School merged with the Englewood School for Boys in 1973. It later housed the mathematics department. It was razed in 1994 to make way for Drapkin Hall, currently home of the Lower School.

Dwight House, in the foreground (right), was built in 1893. Dwight Cottage (far left) was purchased in 1900, and the gymnasium (between the two) built two years later.

1898: The first issue of *Dwightonia*, the Dwight literary magazine, appeared. It would be published continuously until 1949.

1900s

1900: The Cottage, near Dwight House, was purchased for use by boarders. The building was razed in 1955, soon after boarding was phased out.

1902: The Dwight School gymnasium, which also served as a theater, was built, originally accommodating boarders upstairs. In 1982, the building was remodeled as the Swartley Arts Center, home for all visual arts classes.

1902: For the first time, Dwight's entire graduating class went on to college: six to Vassar, two to Smith, and one to Wellesley.

1903: The first Senior Dance was held in February. For years, dresses had to be approved in advance by Misses Creighton and Farrar.

Dwight Hall was added by purchase in 1906, completing the early campus.

Victorian comfort was the order of the day for Dwight boarders in the early years of the twentieth century, as in this dormitory room, where banner and pennant show male alliances.

The living room/library at Dwight House.

1905: Dwight's first student government was formed.

1906: A nearby residence, to be called Dwight Hall, was purchased for classrooms.

1908: The first Dwight yearbook, called *The Record*, was published. It continued until the United States entered World War I in 1917. From then through 1948, the June issue of *Dwightonia* served that function.

The reading room in Dwight Hall, part of the campus from 1906 to 1931.

The entire Dwight campus prior to 1931. From the top to the bottom are Dwight Hall, Dwight House, the gymnasium, and Dwight Cottage.

Senior Field Day was a longstanding tradition at Dwight. This is the 1935 version, with mascot Geoffrey Bear leading the way.

1909: Dwight held its first Senior Field Day, an event that continued through the 1960s.

1910s

1917: Two Dwight seniors bought a truck and transported it to France. Driving it themselves, they offered food and clothing to poor families.

1920s

1922: The first Dwight Christmas Pageant, complete with pantomime and minstrels bearing a boar's head, was held. Three years later, the tradition of seniors carrying candles and singing "Emmanuel" to introduce the Pageant began. In 1930, tableaux based on paintings were introduced, continuing until the Pageant ended in 1976.

1923: The Pinero School, a small elementary school for boys, was founded in a rented house at 35 Dwight Place in Englewood, next to the First Presbyterian Church. In 1928, Pinero would sell the goodwill and some furniture to a new corporation, which would become the Englewood School for Boys, for $1,000.

1923: Two seniors, Consuelo Lee (a boarder from Puerto Rico) and Ethel Robertson, collaborated to write the first two verses and music for the song that was to become the Dwight alma mater. Miss Creighton would write the last verse.

1925: Misses Creighton and Farrar transferred the formerly proprietary (i.e., for-profit) Dwight School to a board of trustees as a gift, and a charter was granted to the school as a non-profit institution.

The 1930 Dwight Christmas Pageant.

Dancing the maypole at the Dwight Junior School.

1927: Dwight Junior School, second through sixth grade, was established in the former home of Dr. Robert Speer on the corner of Brayton and Walnut streets. A few years later, first and pre-primary grades were added, making it possible to enter Dwight at three and graduate "college-ready." This property was sold to the Bede School in 1972 when Dwight closed its Junior School.

Albert Metzger joined the ESB faculty in the school's second year.

1928: Upon the death of Miss Creighton in March, Frances Leggett (Class of 1896) and Maud Jackson Hulst (Class of 1894), both of whom were Dwight teachers a well as alumnae, were appointed co-principals of Dwight School. Miss Hulst would serve until 1947 and Miss Leggett until 1948.

MAUD JACKSON HULST (Class of 1894)

"Maud's figure was abundant, her face like a cherub with character, and her heart warm and loving. She could have well said 'let me live by the side of the road and be a friend to man.'" *Dorothy Rowley Brockie '09, in the Spring 1985* Dwight Bulletin.

FRANCES LEGGETT (Class of 1896)

"To all that knew her she represented the best of womanhood and the embodiment of the highest human qualities—dignity, patience, courage, understanding, selflessness, and faith." *From Miss Leggett's memorial service.*

1928: Englewood School for Boys—often referred to as "ESB" or "Englewood School" or "the Boys' School"—was founded by a board of trustees as a non-profit institution on the Pinero School property at 35 Dwight Place. Fifty students in grades three through ten began studying with six teachers under the direction of Headmaster Robert T. Hall, who served until 1934. Among the six was E. Butler Beaumont, who would stay for forty-five years, the entire span of ESB. (In the last decade of the nineteenth century there had been an unrelated Englewood School for Boys.) Eventually the second floor of the Dwight Place property's barn would be converted into an art studio and woodworking shop, and a thirty-by-sixty-foot "demountable" (moveable) four-room building would be added in 1929 for the Junior School. This classroom building was later moved to the 363 Palisade Avenue property, where it would serve as a gymnasium.

ROBERT T. HALL

"Headmaster Hall put first things first and promptly went about engaging a strong faculty…. He set up a firm college preparatory curriculum, and had the young school approved by both the Department of Instruction of the State of New Jersey and the Middle States Association of

Colleges and Secondary Schools." *From the reflections of Marshall Umpleby, who succeeded Mr. Hall as headmaster.*

1929: In November, ESB students visited the construction site of the George Washington Bridge, then known as the Hudson River Bridge. When it opened to traffic in 1931, it would change the demographics of the Englewood area and boost enrollment at ESB.

1930s

1931: A new "Main Recitation Building" (which would be dedicated in 1964 as Leggett Hall to honor the former headmistress) housing classrooms, laboratories, an auditorium, and a library for the sixth through twelfth grades was completed in July. Now surplus, the former recitation

The Englewood School for Boys in 1931 at its original Dwight Place location. Headmaster Robert Hall is at the center.

ESB gym classes were held at the adjacent First Presbyterian Church throughout the school's time on Dwight Place.

Maud Hulst and Frances Leggett, here in their office in the building that would be named for Miss Leggett, led Dwight for two decades.

Dwight's "Main Recitation Building," later called Leggett Hall, in a hand-colored print.

building, Dwight Hall, was sold. Leggett Field, next to the new building, was completed two years later and would be used for field hockey, baseball, and Field Day.

1931: ESB's first graduating class had two students. The other seventy-four boys attended the graduation at the First Presbyterian Church. By 1933, there were seven in the graduating class.

1932: The Depression hit ESB hard, with teachers forgoing salary increases and helping out with maintenance. Most boys were on partial scholarship, as were many Dwight girls.

1932: Boys from ESB took science classes on the Dwight campus, but not with the girls.

1934: Marshall L. Umpleby was appointed headmaster of ESB. He would lead the school to academic and athletic excellence until his retirement in 1965.

MARSHALL UMPLEBY

"Marshall L. Umpleby is the proud skipper of our fine ship. Since his commission he has had to weather many storms but has always stuck by his post. On this Twentieth Anniversary Mr. Umpleby should be congratulated since he has just brought his ship through its worst passage, World War II, and is again sailing on calm waters. Despite all the storms and hardships, our skipper has made this ship one of the best." *From* Englewood Tradition, *published in 1947.*

1937: When the landlord at 35 Dwight Place balked at the school's erecting another building on the property, ESB moved its classrooms and offices to a rented property at 363 East Palisade Avenue adjacent to Dwight School; the school would purchase it in 1946. The house remained in use through the middle 1960s, ultimately as Lower School classrooms and a lunchroom. The property's stable would become the Upper School classroom building and was later used by the visual arts.

Englewood School at 363 East Palisade Avenue; the stable is visible through the porte cochere.

The stable at 363 East Palisade became the main Upper School classroom building. Behind it is the relocated "demountable" building, now the gymnasium.

The graduating class of 1938, the first at ESB's new location, is decked out in blazers and white ducks.

This view of the complete ESB campus at the time shows that the field has been graded and goalposts and bleachers erected.

1937: The ESB football team was undefeated, untied, and un-scored-upon.

1939: For the first time, Dwight and ESB co-presented a play, *The Swan*. Though school-related adults continued for a time to play women in ESB plays and Dwight girls masqueraded as men in their productions, the ice had been broken, and in later years the schools routinely supplied actors for each other's productions.

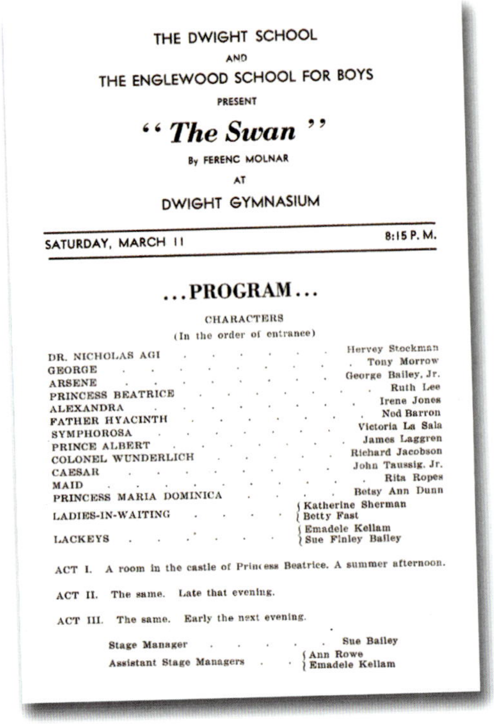

THE DWIGHT SCHOOL
AND
THE ENGLEWOOD SCHOOL FOR BOYS
PRESENT
"The Swan"
By FERENC MOLNAR
AT
DWIGHT GYMNASIUM

SATURDAY, MARCH 11 — 8:15 P. M.

...PROGRAM...

CHARACTERS
(In the order of entrance)

DR. NICHOLAS AGI	Hervey Stockman
GEORGE	Tony Morrow
ARSENE	George Bailey, Jr.
PRINCESS BEATRICE	Ruth Lee
ALEXANDRA	Irene Jones
FATHER HYACINTH	Ned Barron
SYMPHOROSA	Victoria La Sala
PRINCE ALBERT	James Laggren
COLONEL WUNDERLICH	Richard Jacobson
CAESAR	John Taussig, Jr.
MAID	Rita Ropes
PRINCESS MARIA DOMINICA	Betsy Ann Dunn
LADIES-IN-WAITING	Katherine Sherman Betty Fast
LACKEYS	Emadele Kellam Sue Finley Bailey

ACT I. A room in the castle of Princess Beatrice. A summer afternoon.

ACT II. The same. Late that evening.

ACT III. The same. Early the next evening.

Stage Manager	Sue Bailey
Assistant Stage Managers	Ann Rowe Emadele Kellam

Playbill for *The Swan*.

1939: Dwight School celebrated the fiftieth anniversary of the naming of the school, and certain alumnae funded various projects. "There is lots of enthusiasm over the tennis tournament this year. No doubt it is our new extra special 50th Anniversary Fund tennis courts," according to the June *Dwightonia*. The courts were south of Leggett Hall, where the Klein Campus Center now stands.

1940s

1941: ESB produces its first yearbook, *Blue and White.*

1946: Dwight School was accepted into the Cum Laude Society, which had been established in 1908 in emulation of the college-level Phi Beta Kappa Society. Several girls who had graduated in 1945 were made charter members, along with some faculty.

1947: ESB purchased the DeWitt property at 34 North Woodland Street. The building was named Alumni House in appreciation of parents of alumni and alumni themselves who made this possible and was modified to serve school needs: as science classroom and lab, offices, headmaster's (and later development director's) residence, and finally as faculty housing. The building was razed in 2012. The property's garage was moved adjacent to the gymnasium and dedicated in 1948 as Memorial Field House, honoring the eight ESB alumni lost in World War II. Later the building became a library and, finally, a bookstore.

1948: On Miss Leggett's retirement, Marjorie French was appointed headmistress of Dwight School, serving until 1951.

Students walk down the hill from Alumni House after attending science class.

MARJORIE FRENCH

"Her tireless energy, the improvements she has accomplished in our curriculum, her basic personal integrity, and her sincere desire to achieve the best for the school and our students have been fully recognized and appreciated." *From a letter to parents from Blake Wilcox, president of the board of trustees.*

1948: Dwight discontinued its boarding program, at the same time moving from a short school day (with students returning home for lunch) to a full country day school program lasting until midafternoon.

1950s

1950: Groundbreaking ceremonies were held for Hulst House, named for former headmistress Maud Hulst. The building, an annex of what would later be called Leggett Hall, was and is used for meetings, guest lectures, and special student presentations.

1950: ESB purchased from Nathan Solomon at cost the 6.25-acre property a short distance from the school on North Woodland Street, which would be developed as the "Upper Field."

1950: Dwight's newspaper, *The Penton*, was first published in March.

1950: Dwight and ESB began sharing some classrooms and offices.

1952: Marjorie H. Applegate succeeded Miss French as headmistress of Dwight School, serving until 1960.

MARJORIE APPLEGATE

"Greater than responsibility towards parents or school is responsibility towards yourself. You have to live with yourself for many years. It is your responsibility to make those years better by developing your character, your mind and your spirit." *From an editorial by Marjorie Applegate.*

1954: ESB established a chapter of the Cum Laude Society.

1955: The groundbreaking in January for the ESB "Auxiliary," also known as the activities building, marked the first significant new construction ever for ESB. Though most called it "the gym," it also had a stage and was home to ESB's outstanding drama program. After renovation and refurbishment in 2000, the building was renamed in memory of Richard Silberfein '81.

1958: As America raced to overcome the Russians following *Sputnik*, ESB established its first Advanced Placement courses in science. Five years later, the school held its first Science Fair, an event which continued annually until 1971.

Groundbreaking for the ESB "Auxiliary," or activities building. Headmaster Marshall Umpleby holds the shovel.

Hulst House is dedicated in 1950.

Helen Nichol Fernald (left), headmistress of Dwight; Marshall Umpleby, headmaster of ESB; and Constance Chilton, who headed the Elisabeth Morrow School. The Three School Development Foundation was formed to raise funds for these institutions.

1960s

1960: Helen Nichol Fernald was appointed headmistress of Dwight School, serving until 1965.

HELEN NICHOL FERNALD

"The standards here are excellent and there is a beautiful spirit evident in the children and their parents." *Helen Nichol Fernald, from an interview early in her tenure.*

1960: For the first time, girls from Dwight played in the ESB orchestra, renamed the Dwight-Englewood Orchestra.

1962: The Three School Development Foundation was established in April by Dwight School, the Englewood School for Boys, and the Elisabeth Morrow School to raise funds for improvements. Umpleby Hall, Generoso Pope Science Hall, the Lawrence Dining Center, and the Lillian Pitkin Schenck Auditorium were all funded by the Three School Development Foundation in the 1960s. With the merger of Dwight and ESB in 1973, the Foundation became inactive.

1963: The Bede School—named for the Venerable Bede, a historian, writer, and monk from the Middle Ages—opened as a preschool for three- to five-year-olds on the campus of Fairleigh Dickinson University in Teaneck, becoming the first accredited Montessori school in New Jersey. When it outgrew its space at Fairleigh Dickinson, the school moved to the Masonic Hall in downtown Englewood.

1965: The first issue of Dwight's *The Forum* appeared. Its purpose was "to stimulate thought and controversy within the student body by presenting interesting feature articles and critical analysis of school situations."

1965: Margery Day Hanson was appointed headmistress of Dwight School, serving until 1970.

MARGERY DAY HANSON

"She has been uncompromising in her stand on personal honor, responsibility, and personal duty to oneself and society; and by her example has strengthened all those—students, faculty, administration, parents, alumnae, friends, and trustees—who make up the Dwight family in their pursuit.... We all will miss her, but we and Dwight will long bear her mark." *F. F. Taussig '40, president of the board of trustees.*

1965: Mr. Umpleby retired as headmaster of ESB after thirty-five years at the school, thirty as headmaster, and the board appointed Dr. Roger Cooley as his successor. He remained in the position until the Dwight School-ESB merger in 1973, at which time he became director of development.

DR. ROGER COOLEY

"I have developed a deep sense of respect for his humanity, sense of justice, seriousness of purpose, patience and dedication, as well as an appreciation of his good nature and unfailing good will." *Karl Zimmermann '61, from "A Farewell to Dr. Cooley" upon Cooley's retirement.*

1965: By student vote, the official nickname of ESB teams was changed from "Hilltoppers" to "Bulldogs," possibly at the encouragement of Carlos Henriquez, athletic director, physical education teacher, and coach of wrestling, track, and cross-country. His prize dog, Ace, became the mascot. Dwight-Englewood teams remain the Bulldogs.

1965: Umpleby Hall, built where ESB had once planted a World War II "victory garden," was

ESB's Umpleby Hall was funded by the Three School Development Foundation.

dedicated. The building held offices and classrooms from the beginning and is now home to the Middle School.

1966: A fire in the upper floor of Hulst House damaged two art rooms.

1966: The Lillian Pitkin Schenk Auditorium opened for use by both Dwight and ESB for assemblies and theater productions as well as the cafeteria, also shared by the schools. That same year the Pope Science Hall opened on the site once occupied by ESB's academic facility at 363 East Palisade Avenue. Used by both ESB and Dwight, Pope was gender-segregated by floor and had two separate entrances, one for boys and one for girls.

Hulst House art rooms ravaged by fire.

ESB's 363 Palisade building is razed to make room for Pope Science Hall.

The Foundation also funded the science building (left), auditorium, and cafeteria.

Marshall Umbleby speaks at his retirement dinner in 1965.

1968: The Three School Development Foundation purchased Graham House and Graham Field from the Van Alstyne family for faculty housing and reading and acting classes. Graham House now houses the business, admissions, and development offices, and Graham Field is used for girls' field hockey and lacrosse.

1970s

1970: Bede added a primary department for sixteen five- through nine-year-olds to its preschool program, accommodating the new students at the Presbyterian Church at Knickerbocker Road and Demarest Avenue in Englewood.

The ESB campus, including the foreground buildings shared with Dwight, at its fullest extent.

Graham House in spring.

1970: Harold F. Witman was appointed head of Dwight School, serving until the merger in 1973.

HAROLD F. WITMAN

"The Alumnae Board of Dwight School wishes to express its appreciation to Mr. Harold Witman, Headmaster, for his tireless work to maintain and strengthen Dwight School.... We salute him for his faithfulness, endurance, and outstanding organizational ability. We remember with gratitude his concern for each student's academic progress." *Spring 1973* Alumnae Bulletin.

1970: Senior Projects, a precursor to today's Senior Focus program, began.

1971: Dwight purchased Phillips House at 401 Walnut Street as a residence for the headmaster.

1971: Dwight Junior School closed its doors, with its students enrolling the next year at the Elisabeth Morrow School, a partner in the Three School Development Foundation with Dwight and ESB. A substantial gift had allowed EMS to expand its facilities to accommodate these additional students. The Bede School purchased the former Junior School property for its first permanent home.

1972: In anticipation of merger, the Dwight and ESB boards of trustees came together as a joint board for the two schools.

1973: Dwight-Englewood was born when ESB and Dwight merged. Dr. Eugene M. Dea was ap-

E. Butler Beaumont, whose career as teacher and administrator spanned the entirety of ESB history, retired at the merger.

Greenhouse on the roof of Pope, in the original plans and built eight years later, in 1974.

pointed Dwight-Englewood's first headmaster, serving until 1978.

DR. EUGENE M. DEA

"Order in all things is desirable and is always preferable to confusion. The quality to think logically and to articulate clearly is more valuable than the ability to form opinions on the basis of feeling and to verbalize them in slang." *From Dr. Dea's "Five Principles of Education."*

1974: A greenhouse was built atop Pope Science Hall.

1976: The Holiday Concert was inaugurated, using some of the half-century-old Christmas Pageant features. The orchestra, drama and dance clubs, and choir performed.

1977: Emily Hewetson was appointed headmistress of the Bede School, serving until 1982.

EMILY HEWETSON

"Bede was a unique school that offered a safe, loving environment that represented the best of child-centered education where all children were accepted, nurtured, and encouraged, wherever they were on their educational journey. The dedicated, creative faculty centered the curriculum, materials, and projects on the interests and talents of the students." *From Emily Hewetson's recollections.*

1978: Dwight-Englewood opened its new athletic complex, which in 2003 would be refurbished and named Modell's Sport Complex.

1978: *Nicholas Nickleby*, adapted from the Dickens novel by Dr. Dea, who also directed the show, with music by Susan Alexander and lyrics by Wade Benjamin, was performed.

1978: Talk II, informal but organized discussion groups for seventh- and eighth-graders, began.

1978: Dr. James B. Van Hoven was appointed headmaster of Dwight-Englewood, serving until 1984.

DR. JAMES B. VAN HOVEN

"'Involvement' is the key word in Dr. Van Hoven's philosophy, one that aptly expresses his enthusiasm for the whole educational process and especially for the sometimes forgotten though supposed beneficiaries of all the educational theories—the students." *From the September 1978* Dwight-Englewood Newsletter.

1979: The Bede School added grades four through six, accommodating them on the third floor of the Walnut Street facility.

Headmaster Eugene Dea in 1977 on the construction site of the new athletic complex.

1980s

1981: Two girls became Bede School's first sixth-grade graduates. Beginning that year, increasing enrollment led the school to rent space at the First Presbyterian Church on Palisade Avenue for grades four through six.

1982: The Dwight School gym was transformed into the Swartley Arts Center, housing art studios, music and art history classrooms, and a gallery.

1982: Marjorie H. Davis was appointed headmistress of the Bede School, serving until 1985.

1983: The Bede School purchased the estate at 420 Booth Avenue from The Community School for classroom space for grades three through six. Preschool through grade two remained at 255 Walnut Street.

1984: Dr. James Edward Van Amburg was appointed head of Dwight-Englewood, serving until 1998.

DR. JAMES EDWARD VAN AMBURG

"I am very proud of what we have achieved. We are miles away from the school portrayed in so many works of literature… where any children whose identities stood outside the mainstream found themselves invisible with their needs ignored." *James Van Amberg in* D-E Today.

1985: Jane Weeks served ably as interim head of the Bede School, earning accolades from the faculty.

1986: Student government initiated a tradition called "Spirit Week" to kick off the new school year. Another innovation was "Blue and White Day," which immediately preceded Homecoming.

Spirit Week madness continues today.

The Bede School buildings at Brayton and Walnut streets and North Woodland Street and Booth Avenue.

1986: David Lilly was appointed headmaster of the Bede School, serving until the school's 1993 merger with Dwight-Englewood.

DAVID LILLY

"There is nothing more important than the education of children. It is the foundation of our future. There is no responsibility greater than that of the teacher who guides the student from childhood into the wonders of the adult world." *David Lilly.*

1987: The Dwight-Englewood Middle School was re-envisioned with a new "cluster system," a four-discipline team of faculty that opened the possibility of interdisciplinary teaching.

1987: In January, the board of trustees announced the Second Century Campaign, with the goal of raising $6 million by 1989, the school's centennial.

1987: Computer science, an ethics program, and community service became Upper School academic requirements. Today all D-E students are required to complete forty hours of community service prior to graduation.

1988: In September, the Imperatore Library, housing reference and study areas, a film projection room, a lounge, and the Coop/Bookstore, was dedicated.

1989: The Nature Sanctuary was created on the D-E campus. It continues to provide an opportunity for hands-on learning and was certified in 2001 by the National Wildlife Federation.

Imperatore Library is dedicated in 1988.

The Nature Sanctuary.

1989: Dwight-Englewood celebrated its 100th anniversary with a full weekend of events and a gala dinner-dance.

1990s

1991: The boys' varsity soccer team became Bergen County champions. The championship game versus Tenafly was named the "High School Soccer Game of the Century" by the *Record* newspaper in 2000.

1992: On February 11, Stephen "Casey" Kutner '92 scored two goals and an assist in ice hockey in a 7-to-6 loss to Newark Eastside, bringing his career totals to 228 goals and 377 points, which surpassed the national high school record of 375.

1993: N.J. SEEDS (Scholars, Educators, Excellence, Dedication, Success), a nonprofit organization, was founded by a group of New Jersey educators including Dr. Van Amberg. N.J. SEEDS

Soccer Coach Chris Schmid gets a ride after winning the "Game of the Century."

continues today, providing educational opportunities for motivated, high-achieving students from low-income families.

1993: The Bede School merged with Dwight-Englewood to become a pre-K through grade twelve institution. Bede's sixth grade became part of the Middle School.

1994: The "Living Wax Museum" was inaugurated by English teacher Robert Carson, with eighth-graders learning about and then taking on the persona of historic or contemporary characters of note and presenting their stories.

1995: MAGIC (the Michael Andrew Glowski Intramural Competition) was instituted as a fund-

Admissions director and English teacher Rob Carson, who created the Living Wax Museum.

Dr. Seuss in the Living Wax Museum.

MAGIC participants.

raiser for financial aid in memory of Michael Glowski '95, who died during his junior year. Today MAGIC is a favorite annual Field Day event for the Upper School.

1996: Drapkin Hall, a new Lower School building where Dwight House once stood, was dedicated, and grades pre-K through six moved there from Booth Avenue and Walnut Street; the latter for many decades had been home to young students, first Dwight's, then Bede's.

1997: D-E hosted its first Middle School Engineering Challenge.

1998: Dr. Ralph E. Sloan was appointed headmaster, serving until 2006.

DR. RALPH E. SLOAN

"I have gathered a treasury of good feelings about the wonderful people of this fine school—faculty and staff, parents, trustees, and especially students.... There really is common ground and good will here where everyone... understands the purposes, the roles, the limitations, and the personal joys of the school." *From Dr. Sloan's inaugural address.*

Bernice Drapkin cuts the ribbon to open Drapkin Hall as Dr. Van Amburg officiates.

The courtyard playground of Drapkin Hall.

The Puppet Parade.

1998: The Lower School began the "Puppet Parade," now a beloved annual event.

2000s

2004: Tablet personal computers were introduced for students in grades six and nine.

2006: The Klein Campus Center was dedicated, featuring "one-click" classrooms, a new home for the Coop and Bookstore, a student center, practice rooms for instrumentalists, a second performing arts stage (Hajjar Auditorium), and teachers' offices. The dining hall was refurbished and renamed the Wharton-Lessin Dining Hall. The performing arts section of the Klein Campus Center officially became the Khubani Performing Arts Center.

2006: Dr. Rodney V. De Jarnett was appointed head of school, a role in which he continues today.

Hajjar Auditorium, Klein's "black box" space, hosts myriad events year-round.

The Klein Campus Center.

Collins House.

DR. RODNEY V. DE JARNETT

"It is a remarkable, exciting time to be involved in schools. A renaissance in education is underway, as research continues to emerge with regard to best practices in teaching and learning, incredible new technologies are continually created, and brain research yields exciting findings about our individual potential. We have the opportunity and obligation to educate our children for their future, not our past, with an ongoing commitment to our mission to 'make it better.'" *Rodney De Jarnett.*

2006–2008: The Lower School began a recycling, organic gardening, and composting program, a cohesive sustainability initiative that today involves all three divisions.

2007: The Taub Technology Center, located on the second floor of the Imperatore Library, opened in the area once occupied by the Coop and Bookstore.

2007: Collins House, 76 North Woodland Street, was built to serve as the residence of the head of school, replacing Phillips House.

2008: The "Bogo Room," an informal, collaborative student study space, opened in the Imperatore Library. (The family of two D-E students whose grandfather was nicknamed "Bogo" funded the project.)

2010s

2010: The D-E Traveling Orchestra of Upper School students had its first overseas trip, performing in concerts and with other student and professional ensembles in and around London. Now including Middle School students, the orchestra made its second overseas trip in 2013, with performances in Vienna, Prague, and Budapest.

2010: The Leggett-Umpleby Society for older alumni and former faculty and staff was formed and continues today with social events and educational seminars.

2011: The Office of Multicultural Affairs in the Upper School opened, and INSPIRE, a student club dedicated to diversity and multicultural initiatives, began.

2013: The Upper School Ethics Bowl team was invited to the national championships.

2013: D-E Summer Connections had a record-breaking year, attracting nearly 1,000 students in pre-K (age three) through grade twelve for its day camp, enrichment, scholars, and international summer programs.

2013: Research, architectural planning, and fundraising began for the future construction of a new STEM (Science, Technology, Engineering, and Mathematics) building, expected to be completed in 2015.

Day campers with Summer Connections in one of several D-E gardens.

INSPIRE hosts the school's annual Holi Festival of Colors.

A 2013 view of the Dwight-Englewood School campus from the sky.

WHAT AND HOW WE LEARNED

The only constant is change, according to Heraclitus, and in reviewing the history of four schools, the oldest of which began 125 years ago, there's bound to be plenty of that. Change has been especially profound in the demographics of the student body and the physical plant, and the evolution of programs and pedagogy also has also been dramatic. Still, an ongoing tradition of education and its most fundamental goals and objectives remains largely unchanged. This continuing purpose has been the combination of excellent academics with an experience that leads students to more satisfying and productive lives.

"Miss Creighton and Miss Farrar were not only interested in giving their girls a good education, but in fitting them for life," according to long-time Dwight principal Frances Leggett '96, speaking of the school's founders at, appropriately, the 1966 Founders' Day. "Miss Creighton once said, 'It's not life that matters; it's what you put into it.'" Their goals reached beyond simple excellence in academics to the need for students to develop the skills and the desire to contribute to the world around them.

The first mission statement of the Englewood School for Boys (ESB), written in 1932, sounded a similar note: "A non-sectarian institution founded for the purpose of preparing boys to become men through the medium of education—an education which includes advancement in learning, a consciousness of their obligation to society, of which they are members, and an appreciation of the ideals upon which their country was founded, a heritage which they must be able to protect, carry on, and further." The theme of the celebration of the

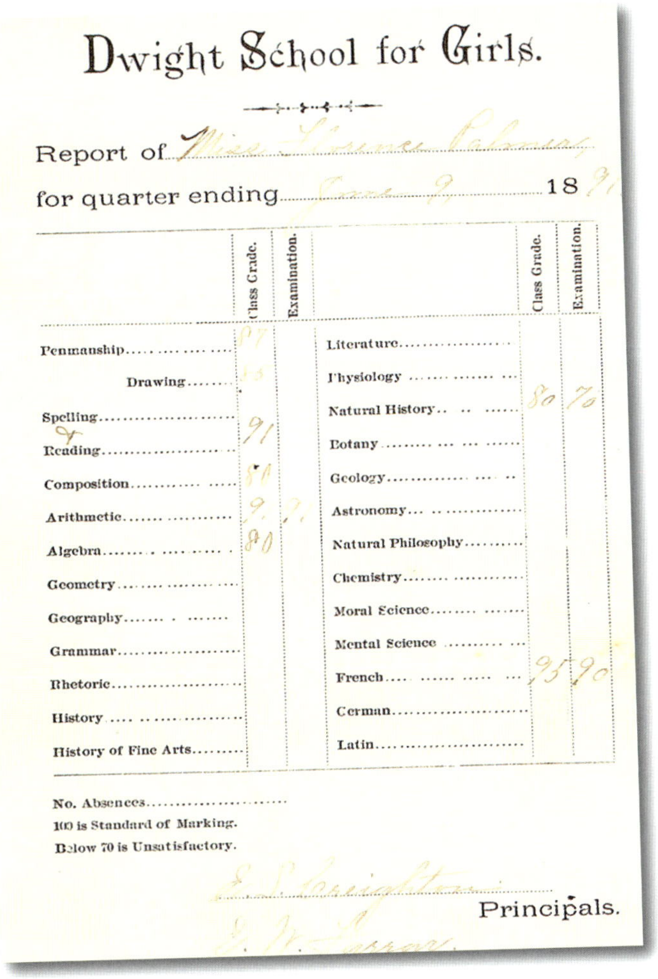

Dwight School for Girls.

Report of Miss Lorence Palmer

for quarter ending June 9 1891

	Class Grade.	Examination.		Class Grade.	Examination.
Penmanship	87		Literature		
Drawing	85		Physiology		
Spelling & Reading	91		Natural History	80	70
Composition	81		Botany		
Arithmetic	9.	7.	Geology		
Algebra	80		Astronomy		
Geometry			Natural Philosophy		
Geography			Chemistry		
Grammar			Moral Science		
Rhetoric			Mental Science		
History			French	95	90
History of Fine Arts			German		
			Latin		

No. Absences

100 is Standard of Marking.

Below 70 is Unsatisfactory.

E. Creighton

E. W. Farrar

Principals.

This "Dwight School for Girls" report card from 1891, signed by the headmistresses Creighton and Farrar, shows a remarkable breadth of curriculum.

Opposite page: Headmistress Maud Hulst teaches art history in 1942.

one-hundredth anniversary of the school in 1989 was "Education for a Just Society." The current Dwight-Englewood mission statement ends, "in order to meet the challenges of a changing world and make it better."

At all three of Dwight-Englewood's predecessor schools, educators consistently have seen the development of strong character as an important educational goal and considered it an essential component of a satisfying and productive life. "Pupils will be urged to cultivate self-respect and self control," the 1889 Dwight catalogue reads, "in short to be self-governing as far as possible." The Englewood School for Boys catalogue for 1936–37 identifies influencing boys "to become citizens of sound character" as one of three critical aims. The Bede School's program was designed around principles that Maria Montessori thought prepared young adults to embrace fully the study of culture and the sciences in order to influence and lead civilization.

Education at all three schools has always included the acquisition of a broad range of knowledge and skills, but with the recognition that only if students have developed the ability to and habit of using knowledge and skills independently can they reach their larger goals. "As a community of learners," the current mission statement opens, "Dwight-Englewood School strives to foster in each student a passion for life-long learning." The first catalogue of Dwight School, written in 1889, articulates as a mission "to so interest pupils that they will learn to love study for its own sake."

Sound physical development was from the beginning a core part of the educational experience at both Dwight and at ESB, which listed in

Basketball was a young sport when Dwight girls began to play, outdoors at first. Here the 1905 team poses with a collie named Commodore.

the 1936–37 catalogue as one of the three aims "to develop healthy bodies." Girls at Dwight were playing "basket-ball" (as it was then written) just a few years after the game was invented by James Naismith in 1891. In the school's earliest years, girls were required to spend one hour every day in physical activity, preferably out of doors, weather allowing.

Educating students for a changing world has been a commitment throughout our 125-year history. Dwight School would prepare girls for one of history's most profound changes, the movement of many more upper- and middle-class women into positions as wage-earners or professionals. In the 1890s, the general expectation remained that young women of the upper classes would be wives, mothers, and social hostesses, yet Miss Creighton and Miss Farrar intended to educate young women for multiple possibilities. In its first year, Dwight offered a course of study leading to automatic "acceptance at Smith or Wellesley without examination." Alternatively, students had a choice of "two carefully planned courses of study, Classical and English," designed to make cultivated and literate women of those who chose lives in the traditional family setting.

All members of the Dwight Class of 1902 went on to college.

Young Englewood School for Boys students are instructed in shop by Theodore McCarthy circa 1933 in the former barn on the school's original campus at 35 Dwight Place.

In 1928, when the Englewood School for Boys was founded and Frances Leggett '96 and Maude Jackson Hulst '94 assumed leadership of Dwight when Miss Creighton died, the Dwight catalogue showed similar but expanded options: a college preparatory program "adapted to meet the admission requirements of the better colleges and universities"; three programs for girls not wishing to attend college but desiring "planned courses of study, extending beyond the college requirements" (a literary course, a scientific course, and a classical course); post-graduate work for "students not wishing to go to college, but who desire to continue their studies" or students needing one additional year of instruction before entering college, and finally a two-year program in the Department of Secretarial Studies that prepared students not only to become assistants to "those engaged in scientific, literary or professional pursuits, but also as training for the management of one's own business."

Dwight for a time offered a two-year program in the Department of Secretarial Studies. These girls are learning to type in a classroom in the Main Recitation Building, now Leggett Hall, in 1941.

The Creighton Memorial Library, in what would become Leggett Hall, offered a comfortable and elegant place for Dwight girls to study. In was named in honor of founding headmistress Euphemia S. Creigton, who appears in bas-relief above the fireplace. The room currently serves as the faculty study.

The varied offerings of programs at Dwight reflected an educational principal important to the school's eponymous Timothy Dwight. As president of Yale University, he reorganized and revised the curriculum, for the first time allowing juniors and seniors to choose electives. Following his educational philosophy, the founders of Dwight School had included a choice of program and subjects from the very beginning. Dr. Rodney De Jarnett, the current head of school, has followed in the footsteps of those Dwight School founders, and of all of the previous heads of Dwight-Englewood. Among his signature programs are the junior/senior electives, which have replaced most requirements.

Travel has always been considered essential to education at the schools. Dwight's 1889 brochure boasted that both founders "had the advantage of extended travel and residence abroad." Prior to World War I, Coeur Dwight was a branch of the school abroad that offered students the opportunity to spend an academic year studying and traveling in Paris and across Europe. The 1928–29 Dwight catalogue listed an Art and Travel Class in which students studied the geography, history, literature, and art of the countries of Europe, with the goal of soon becoming "intelligent and appreciative travelers somewhat independent of Baedeker and Murray." During summers, students in the class could visit Europe with faculty leaders. Recent Dwight-Englewood trips to Spain, Italy, Peru, and Ecuador are in that tradition.

That 1928–29 catalogue also reflects the advantage taken of opportunities offered by New York City. This could as well be a description of the theater trips led by Malcolm Duffy and others in the 1960s and '70s, or such current trips as the fifth-graders' attendance at Metropolitan Opera rehearsals, Middle School trips to the Metropolitan Museum and Museum of Natural History, and Upper School art students' visits to the galleries of the city and walking tours of downtown Manhattan.

The academic situation at the Englewood School for Boys was somewhat different from Dwight's, since all students were expected to be college-bound. Many would attend boarding school after a few preparatory years at ESB, while others would remain until graduation. (As of 1961, then-headmaster Marshall Umpleby noted, 96 percent of the school's 370 graduates had gone to four-year colleges; Princeton topped the list with twenty-nine enrollments.) The core academic program for the former group was set by the Secondary Education Board, which wrote rigorous examinations in English, Latin, mathematics, and French, required for application at the prestigious boarding schools to which ESB students aspired. The program for those remaining until graduation was set by the College Entrance Examination Board, which prepared

Right from the beginning, Dwight School valued travel, both foreign and domestic, as an important part of education. Here a Dwight group poses in 1938 in front of the Capitol Building in Washington.

an equally rigorous set of examinations in those same disciplines. These core programs were narrower and more focused than the opportunities at Dwight. In fact, since science was not required for college entrance, it wasn't taught at the Boys' School until 1931, when one unit of general science was added to the requirements for grade nine. In 1937, when the school moved "up the hill" to 363 East Palisade Avenue, science facilities were created and that discipline became central to the academic program.

For the better part of two decades, ESB's resources, in facilities especially, were limited, a problem exacerbated by the Great Depression and World War II. Mr. Umpleby, headmaster from 1934 to 1965, looked back on the school in those early years as rich in hopes and aspirations, small in size, endowed with an outstanding, dedicated

Dwight girls are learning domestic skills in this late 1940s class held on the second floor of Leggett Hall.

Dwight had particularly modern lab facilities and for a time ESB classes were held there.

Adolph Amend, Jr. supervises two ESB students working in the science lab on the lower level of Alumni House; its acquisition in 1947 finally provided the school with a proper space for science instruction.

This early view of a Dwight classroom shows the lockstep of front-facing desks that remained the norm in education for many decades.

faculty and staff, but limited by circumstances. To the extent possible, however, the academic program was expanded and extracurricular programs, including athletics and dramatics, enhanced.

Photographs from the early years suggest the pedagogy at the time: classrooms of student desks set up in rows, blackboards with notes related to subject matter, students in one-on-one sessions with teachers. Until the 1950s, virtually the only variation on those rows of desks were in science labs and art studios. However, both schools relied on factors still strongly valued today at D-E: small classes, teachers with strong academic preparation in their fields and a devotion to teaching, and close relationships between faculty and students.

Dwight and ESB, as well as the Bede School, share a legacy of teachers and administrators who devoted their lives to their schools. Dwight's first co-principals, the Misses Creighton, Farrar, and Leggett and Mrs. Hulst, led the school from its founding until 1948, almost six decades. In 1933, Beverly Bishop joined the Junior School faculty, remaining for thirty-eight years, the last twenty-six as director of that division. Known as "Miss Junior School," she was called "the golden cord which carried the heritage, traditions, character and structure" of the division. Juliette Gruet taught French for forty years, Anne Meredith Latin for thirty-three, and Marjorie Cannon Bailey '17

Boys are in ties and jackets and desks are in rows in this circa 1950s view of study hall. The study hall was situated in the "demountable" (moveable) building that began as classrooms at ESB's original 35 Dwight Place location and came with the school in 1937 to its new location at 363 Palisade Avenue to serve as a gymnasium. Construction of a new gym in 1955 opened this chameleon-like structure for a new use.

"Classroom" was being more loosely defined by 1964 when Bob Gordon taught this summer-session AP English class in the then Senior Garden of Leggett Hall.

Beverly Bishop, director of the Dwight Junior School for many years, speaks with some of her charges in 1971.

taught religion and Ena Pryde physical education for thirty.

Marshall Umpleby arrived at ESB as a teacher of grades three to six in 1929, one year after its founding, became headmaster in 1934, and remained in that position for thirty-one years. E. Butler Beaumont was among ESB's first-year hires and stayed until the merger, a remarkable forty-five years, every year of the school's independent existence. He was assistant headmaster for thirty of those. Albert Metzger came to the year-old school with a distinguished academic background—a B.A. from Dartmouth and an M.A. from Princeton—and so he and other early hires reinforced at ESB the Dwight practice of attracting teachers with the highest academic credentials. (Robert Hall, founding head of ESB, graduated from Princeton, Mr. Beaumont from Yale, and Mr. Umpleby from Wesleyan.) Metzger too stayed for forty-five years, "a master history teacher" in Umpleby's words. Luke Ward, Umpleby's first appointment as headmaster, remained the heart and soul of athletics at ESB until his retirement in 1959.

Malcolm Duffy came to ESB in 1961 and stayed for forty-seven years, beginning as an English teacher but eventually filling every role imaginable but head of school. He was the longest tenured of all. Among those who started at ESB, Robert Carson was next with forty-three years. On the Dwight side, Rebecca Blackwell Neely served the schools for forty-five years and was joined in the forty-year-plus club by Doris Gelman and Frimi Sagan. Of those who started at the Bede School, Janet Glass, Mary Mesiano, and Joan Sommer were the notable veterans with over twenty-eight years of service when they retired.

With the exception of the shifting role of women, the period from 1889 to the end of World War II had seen only slow and incremental societal changes, and Dwight School and Englewood School for Boys reflected that. Soon after World War II, however, the pace of change picked up and has continued to accelerate until the present day. But at both schools it was for a time more measured than headlong.

Edie Lauderdale, seen here conferring with a student, was assistant head of Dwight and then Dwight-Englewood. The Edith Rotch Lauderdale Professional Day, funded through her generosity, began in 1990 and for years brought visiting speakers to campus annually for faculty enrichment.

"Dwight seeks to be neither progressive nor conservative in the true sense of the word," Headmistress Marjorie Applegate wrote to Dwight parents in 1951. "We are progressive in the sense that we seek to develop the individual child, that we endeavor to keep abreast of the newest techniques in pedagogy, and that we seek constantly to offer a variety of courses best suited for the child of the present era. We are conservative in the sense that we demand self-discipline of our students, that we expect teacher planning rather than student initiative of the material of our curriculum, and that we believe there are certain human verities that must be taught to all children regardless of the era in which they live."

"Our faith in a conservative curriculum does not mean that we are opposed to change," reads the ESB mission statement from 1961. "Indeed, there is no complacent department in the School. Each element within it—administrative, academic, athletic, extracurricular—seeks by experiment, by change of materials and presentation, and by new ideas to improve its work."

As Edie Lauderdale, assistant head of the merged school, wrote in 1978, "The curricula for the high school years in both schools changed little, and graduation requirements not at all until the '60s." One kind of change had been coming, however, though slowly.

"A further development, which has gained momentum since 1950," Mr. Umpleby wrote in 1952, "is the sharing of both instructional and staff facilities with the Dwight School." With the merger still many years away, girls were already studying physics, advanced mathematics, and mechanical drawing at ESB and boys were taking advanced French at Dwight and expanding their language choices with Spanish there. Plays presented by either school included students from the other. "Altogether," according to Mr. Umpleby, "these experiences in co-education have been happy ones for all concerned, and the possibilities of further relationships are limited only by such practical considerations as teacher-loading and working space." Probably no one reading these comments then would have anticipated that twenty years later the schools would publish a joint Course Offerings booklet, a major step toward the merger planned for the following year.

Another major change just prior to the merger was the modular schedule shared by both schools. Crafted by Ms. Lauderdale, it challenged the long-held notion that academic time should be organized into a day divided into equal blocks of time, with subjects meeting at the same time every day of the week. In the new schedule periods varied from twenty-seven minutes to one hour. Classes didn't meet at the same time every day of the week nor for the same length of time.

The explosion in course offerings which began as the schools merged didn't come simply from the doubling of school size.

Dwight and ESB shared faculty and facilities in a limited way long before the 1973 merger, with boys attending science classes at Dwight as early as 1932. Here ESB students learn typing in the 1960s.

"One of the distinguishing features of this new school is the change that has occurred in the areas of arts, athletics, and activities," according to Bruce Smith, then the dean of boys and now a nationally known poet. "The fourth 'A,' academics, continues as the rigorous college preparation of both schools. Meanwhile, course offerings have become broader and more various."

Over time in the years following the merger, Upper School faculty added programs giving students a new role in their education. A service requirement exposed students to a broad range of experiences of their own choosing and promoted reflection on them. An independent study program let students identify academic topics of particular interest outside the regular curriculum for faculty-led study. Senior projects encouraged students to identify interests, academic or real world, to explore.

Talk II and PGM—Peer Group Meeting—were developed after several crises in the Middle School alerted faculty to the need to pay more attention to the social development of students during those years. In response, Ms. Lauderdale; Mayo Schramm, Middle School principal; and Nancy Robin Jaicks '55, a history teacher, created Talk II, a program that had Upper School students (joined by faculty volunteers) serving as group discussion leaders and role models for their younger peers, at first seventh-graders. Topics were selected in a weekly meeting of students and teachers based on the needs and interests of seventh-graders. The selection process for student leaders was careful and intensely competitive. Next came the eighth-grade PGM program, with students beginning to lead discussions without the constant presence of faculty.

Prior to the merger, both schools had experimented with interdisciplinary courses. As Upper School principal at D-E, Gene Wojtyla expanded this concept in her division just as the Middle School was making interdisciplinary teaching a key component of its revamped program. Ms. Gelman and Ms. Sagan initiated an interdisciplinary English and history course, while mathematics and science began coordination efforts that would lead to the MST (Math, Science, Technology) program in the '90s.

Beginning in the early '80s, Rebecca Blackwell, head of the Middle School, led a far-reaching and visionary effort to remake that division. The first major change was the separation to the degree possible of the teaching faculties of the Middle and Upper schools. For the first time the Middle School would be staffed by teachers who shared the same thorough academic preparation as their Upper School colleagues but also understood the special needs of and preferred to work with this age group.

Becky Blackwell, here in her classroom, engineered great change and improvement during her tenure as head of the Middle School.

Middle School students range widely in both physical development and the ability to do abstract thinking. Furthermore, multiple studies show that they tend to compartmentalize what they learn and lose the habit of thinking across disciplines, a constraint to independent thinking. Thus interdisciplinary courses would be important, and the wide span of physical and intellectual development would require flexibility in class times and group sizes. To this day, a team of four teachers—English, social studies, math, and science—shares the same group of students and the same periods of teaching time, arranged in large blocks stretching across multiple back-to-back periods, an arrangement which allows maximum flexibility. They can teach single-discipline classes or plan interdisciplinary units that involve multiple subjects.

The Blue Ribbon Schools program, an initiative under the joint aegis of the United States Department of Education and the National Association of Secondary School Principals, had been created to bring to the nation's attention model schools worthy of study and emulation. In 1987, Dwight-Englewood was honored under the program as an exemplary "Blue Ribbon" secondary school. Dr. Van Amburg and Ms. Wojtyla, who was most responsible for reshaping the Upper School curriculum, had traveled to Washington, D.C., to receive the award from President Ronald Reagan and Secretary of Education William Bennett.

Robert Brisk '76 followed Ms. Wojtyla as principal of the Upper School. During a tenure marked by the continuing change envisioned by Dr. Van Amburg and then supported under his successor, Dr. Ralph Sloan, he brought a second important national recognition to the school, this time for the school's innovative Senior Focus program. Expanding upon the principles underlying the Senior Project, the course allowed students to identify an interest and pursue its study independently.

Seniors in this program spent (and still spend today) the first semester in a small group supervised by one teacher, but each doing independent academic research and producing a paper. In the second semester they drop some courses to do fieldwork under the supervision of an expert from outside the school. This leads to a portfolio and presentation before a knowledgeable panel. In 2003, the National Association of Independent Schools honored D-E with the Leading Edge Award for Curriculum Innovation for this program. From among 701 eligible schools, over 250 programs applied for the award and only a very few were recognized as "stellar examples of what NAIS member schools are doing right."

As the ethnic diversity of the student body increased beginning in the '60s, and at an accelerating pace ever since, the curriculum had to respond. Under the leadership of Ms. Gelman and then Carole DeVito, who succeeded her as history department chair, their department was the first to substantially revamp offerings at most grade levels. Ms. Gelman won for D-E two of the first

National Endowment for the Humanities grants awarded to a high school, funds which allowed fifteen teachers to study the history of India, China, Japan, and the nations of Islam.

When Dr. De Jarnett became head of school, expansion of course choices, initially in the junior and senior years, continued a direction vigorously initiated by Dr. Van Amberg and supported by Dr. Sloan: moving the curriculum beyond the Western tradition at many grade levels and across many disciplines. Sixth-graders by now studied the Near East and Egypt, seventh-graders the traditional societies of China and Africa, and eighth-graders could elect a global studies and citizenship course. Ninth- and tenth-grade history was taught with a world focus. In their junior and senior years, students could choose from a plethora of non-Western electives in the English, social studies, language, ethics, and arts departments.

When Peter Davies moved into the position of assistant head of school, he joined John King, then as now chair of the department of mathematics, and Don McNeil, then chair of the science department, to create the MST program, integrating and reordering the subdisciplines of math, science, and technology in grades nine through eleven in a more logical progression. Now mastery of the basics of technology was required of all students, no matter their background and initial level of interest. This process of evolutionary change continues, as current faculty plan for the programs that will move into an innovative new STEM (Science, Technology, Engineering, and Mathematics) facility, anticipated to be completed by the fall of 2015.

Thus technology will continue to play an ever more dramatic role in the revolution of pedagogy, and revolutionary it seems in comparison to the early years. Rows of desks are largely gone. Desks in circles or "U" shapes have been common since the '60s and remain in use, but today's students are likely to be gathered around a large Harkness table or seated on moveable chairs in groups of two, four, or six—any number engaged in collaborative work. This is part of the move from a teacher-centered classroom to a more student-centered classroom.

Harkness tables provide a setting conducive to today's student-centered classroom.

Ms. Gelman neatly summed up this evolution in pedagogy. The first half of her career saw teachers seeking to identify their own individual "style of teaching," she said, while in the second half teachers concentrated on understanding the individual "learning styles" of their students.

THE PLAY'S THE THING

Records show that plays were first presented at Dwight from its earliest days: *As You Like It* in 1892, *Twelfth Night* in 1918, and *Much Ado about Nothing* in the 1920–21 school year. Theater was always important at the Englewood School for Boys (ESB), too. In 1935, for example, third- and fourth-graders appeared in *The Alo Man*, and in 1938, John Drinkwater's *Abraham Lincoln* had a cast of forty, including faculty, faculty wives, and students' mothers. "A sweeping success," *The Spectator*, the Boys' School student newspaper, called it. Starting in 1939, ESB students began to appear in Dwight plays and Dwight girls in ESB productions.

At ESB and then D-E from 1946 until 1976, English teacher Fred B. Hutchins directed many plays, including *The Taming of the Shrew* in 1948. Another highlight was the 1959 production of Arthur Miller's *The Crucible*. In June of that year, eighteen ESB students and ten Dwight girls presented to great acclaim the climactic trial scene from that play at the National Thespian Society Conference at Indiana University. A few years later, Mr. Hutchins became president of that (then international) organization.

In the spring of 1961, Alexandra "Lex" Stavrou '63 appeared in Hutchins's production of *The Teahouse of the August Moon*. "Mr. Hutchins hammered into us that, no matter what, we had to stay concentrated in our roles," Ms. Stavrou commented. "It's a lesson that I still use in my teaching." In 1964, to mark the four-hundredth anniversary of Shakespeare's birth, Hutchins directed *The Merchant of Venice*, again on the stage in the ESB gym-activities building (now the Silberfein Gym). The memorable Bassanio was Paul Sammarco '66.

As You Like It (1892)

Opposite page: *Twelfth Night* (1918)

"ESB represented my first introduction to stage productions," Mr. Sammarco has said. "It gave me a lot of confidence that I needed to perform on stage, and I've had to do quite a bit of that over the past fifty years."

Also in *Merchant* was Benjamin Gerson '65, a fine Antonio. "Being a shy fifteen-year-old," Mr. Gerson said, "it never occurred to me to try out for a school play. But Mr. Hutchins had other ideas. Also, being in a school play did offer a collateral benefit: it was just about the only chance for us boys to get within fifty feet of a Dwightie."

In 1966, for the first production in the new Lillian Pitkin Schenck Auditorium with its revolving stage, the Captain Vere in *Billy Budd* was Mr.

The Taming of the Shrew (1948)

The stage crew constructs the set for *The Merchant of Venice* (1964).

Sammarco, who remembers not only his cast mates but also "the amazing work" of the stage crew, supervised for the last time by Bill and Jane Oliphant. On stage crew that year was Jay Lesenger '69, now a prominent opera stage director.

In the late 1960s and early '70s, ESB plays—including *Nobody Loves an Albatross, Queens of France*, and *The Sandbox*—were staged by Malcolm Duffy. In 1971, Christopher Soldo '72 appeared in *The Playroom*. "In retrospect, it was a rather mature play for a high school," Mr. Soldo noted. "I don't know if it went over well with the parents. Still, it sealed my fate. I was never going to be an actor again but chose instead to work behind-the-scenes, in film."

In 1959, at Dwight, Laurel Chenet Zimmermann '62, new to the school, was cast by Marion Edwards as the female lead in *Father of the Bride*. "Arriving as a very green freshman," Ms. Zimmermann commented, "I was clueless about activities and fell into the drama club for no particular reason. However, I spent four happy years acting and doing technical work on the stage in the old Dwight gym (now the Swartley Arts Center), and those experiences have spawned a love of all aspects of theater ever since."

Nobody Loves an Albatross (1969)

"My passion for theater began in my student days at the Dwight School," wrote Carla Maria Verdino-Süllwold '65, who years later taught at Dwight and then D-E. "I appeared in every production at both Dwight and ESB. I was privileged to learn my craft from Fred Hutchins, ably assisted by Malcolm Duffy, and Martha Robinson. Bitten by the 'bug,' I went on to a concentration in theater at Sarah Lawrence College."

Martha Robinson directed Ms. Verdino-Süllwold in the lead role in *Murder in a Nunnery* at Dwight and later, at D-E, staged plays like *The Rivals* and *The Swan*. Ms. Robinson (at the school from 1960 to 1980) also had a cameo in the D-E musical *Nicholas Nickleby*. Even today, former students like Stefan Bucek '75 and Paul Lucas '79 remember her fondly as both a person and director. "What a difference a person like Martha can make in another's life," Mr. Lucas has said.

The Skin of Our Teeth (1974)

D-E's first head of school, Dr. Eugene Dea, with Joseph Erwin at the piano, introduced musicals for the first time, directing four of the first five. First up was *Guys and Dolls*, with its large cast of students and some faculty. In an ensemble role was a new faculty member and coach, Vince deLalla. "What I liked best about the show, besides the applause, was what I liked about teaching and coaching: seeing the difference it made in students' lives," Mr. deLalla wrote years later. "Also, the show was a hit, and I felt lucky to be part of it."

In a major *Guys and Dolls* role was teacher Sam Bacon, terrific as Nathan Detroit. "It speaks very well of everyone," Mr. Bacon noted recently, "that they put up with me. I was petrified most of the time and have avoided such shenanigans ever since." Mr. Bacon had replaced a student who had dropped out early in rehearsals.

Guys and Dolls (1975)

Next up—with *South Pacific* and Dr. Dea's own *Nicholas Nickleby* (with Tate Donovan '81 in a supporting role) still to come—was *Oliver!*, with a great set by Ken Cohen, beautifully executed by Ms. Verdino-Süllwold. In the title role was Paul Lucas '79. "When I was a child, no one knew that I could sing," Mr. Lucas said, "and when I arrived at D-E, I knew nothing about musicals or auditioning." Still, his singing of "Happy Birthday" at auditions landed him the lead. "I have been in love with theater ever since," he added, "and have made it my life."

First at ESB and later at D-E in the 1970s, some plays were directed by Carlton Colyer. "My experiences backstage at Schenck led me to my later college choices and then my professional career," Stephen Gambino '75 has commented. "Working with Carla Süllwold, along with support for my photographic endeavors by Karl Zimmermann '61, I had the stepping stones for a great career in entertainment lighting."

Also on stage crew in those days was Mark Overton '75, now head carpenter at *Wicked* on Broadway. After his work on shows at D-E, including Mr. Colyer's staging of *Our Town*, in which he also played the silent role of Farmer McCarthy, Mr. Overton went off to Emerson College as a design major. "Steve Gambino was a big influence in my spending time in the theater," Mr. Overton said, "as were teachers like Fred Hutchins and Malcolm Duffy, both through academics and their presence in and around school productions."

One of Mr. Colyer's very best productions was Thornton Wilder's *The Skin of Our Teeth*. Sabina was Susan Devine-Lempert '74. "I have many fond memories of my years in theater at Dwight, ESB, and then D-E," she recalled. "Sabina was a huge highlight of my 'career' at D-E. Carlton Colyer was a great director. Also, Malcolm Duffy, whose knowledge and love of theater was always inspirational, taught a great senior year class in which a group of us studied scripts and then went on field trips to see what seemed like dozens of professional productions in and around New York City."

Gene Dea, Carla Süllwold, and Malcolm Duffy study the script for a mid-'70s spring musical.

Building on the rich tradition of the earlier D-E productions, Technical Director Leon Di Leone, who arrived at D-E in 1979, gave directors additional support. Mr. Di Leone, still at D-E thirty-five years later, introduced state-of-the-art lighting and a soundboard, a rigging system for lights and scenery, and a stagecraft shop to build more elaborate sets.

In the 1980s, an important member of the stage crew was Daniel Fish '85, now a prominent stage director. "To me," Mr. Fish said, "making theater is now very much as it was when I was at D-E: an opportunity to tell stories that might not otherwise get heard, to learn about and to reveal something about human nature."

The 1980s saw many memorable D-E theater performances. Marc Wolf '80, who many years later won an Obie for his own play, *Another American: Asking and Telling*, shared in *Finian's Rainbow* the role of Finian with Mike Giancarlo '80. Joey Langer '84 appeared in the musicals *Dear World*, *The Boys from Syracuse*, and *Oliver!*. Michael Leiter '87, years later the director of the National Counterintelligence Center, was Tevya in *Fiddler on the Roof*. The force behind most of these shows was the truly dynamic duo of Brian Aschinger and Ann Crawford.

A prominent D-E play director in the 1980s was Norwegian-born Martin Nordal, whose productions included *Six Characters in Search of an Author* and *The Crucible*. In several of Mr. Nordal's productions (including *She Stoops to Conquer* and *The Prime of Miss Jean Brodie*) was Mira Sorvino '85, who played the female lead opposite Mr. Langer in Woody Allen's *Play It Again, Sam*. Years

Play It Again, Sam (1984)

later, Ms. Sorvino won an Oscar for her role in Allen's 1995 film *Mighty Aphrodite*.

Many D-E Middle School productions in the 1980s were staged by Greg Cummings. Highlights included *2004: Welcome to the Future* and *A Midsummer Night's Dream*, the latter production also touring to the Masters School in Dobbs Ferry, New York. Costumes for several of the Nordal and Cummings shows were designed by French teacher Anita Liskin, who had assisted with costumes for the first Broadway production of *On the Town*.

Toward the close of the decade there were two plays staged by Scottish-born Jane Sharp, wife of ESB alumnus John Cornet '54. First came Eugene O'Neill's *Ah, Wilderness!*, with Miriam Sirota '89 as Aunt Lily, and then *Charley's Aunt*, featuring Matt Silverstein '90, years later a professional comedy writer, and Mandy Mishell Hackett '88, now a top administrator at the Public Theater in New York City.

Throughout the 1990s, many other plays and sometimes musicals were also staged by Ms. Sharp. A particular highlight was an adaptation of Dylan Thomas's film script of *The Doctor and the Devils*, set in Edinburgh. "The show," Ms. Sharp has written, "was a nightmare of multiple sets, scenes, and Scottish accents. Full marks go to the

The Man Who Came to Dinner (1996)

The Doctor and the Devils (2007)

Little Me (2002)

student actors, designers, and stage crew who tackled, conquered, and delivered with gusto the true story of the enlightened Dr. Knox."

In 2002 and 2003, Gad Guterman staged the musicals *Little Me* and *Working*. "It was a pleasure," he says, "to work for a school that cared deeply about the performing arts. I had the opportunity to work with very talented students as well as with supportive, gifted colleagues. Each show and each theater class presented particular challenges and joys; all helped me to grow as a teacher and as an artist."

Two *Little Me* performers—Allison Hirschlag '02 and Justin Barad '02—still fondly recall their stage experiences here. "Going head-first in the world," Mr. Barad commented, "would not have been as seamless without the sense of confidence that I developed on the stage at D-E." Ms. Hirschlag, who is still close to many of her *Little Me* cast mates, added, "D-E's theater program is responsible for solidifying those friendship bonds. I for one could not have asked for a better way to grow."

Also in *Little Me* was Dan McCabe '02, son of D-E photography teacher and yearbook advisor John McCabe. A writer and professional actor, McCabe has appeared in plays in Boston, Cambridge, St. Louis, and New York. Especially memorable was his performance as Tom Lee in the Off Broadway revival of *Tea and Sympathy*.

In 2004, Mr. Guterman directed the hilarious production of *A Funny Thing Happened on the Way to the Forum*. Marc Berenson '02, who played Hysterium, still laughs to himself as he recalls the performance. "Gad Guterman—

Godspell (2009)

as well as Jane Sharp, Dan Hughes, and Matt Schukis—all hold a special place in my heart," Mr. Berenson has said, "for helping me grow a talent that, while no longer my main focus, contributes greatly to my ability to stay calm in critical situations and to project a caring bedside manner with patients."

In 2008, Clinton Carbon (now director of multicultural affairs) took on the difficult and challenging *The Laramie Project*, the emotionally charged true story of a young man brutally murdered because of his sexual orientation. "The play," Mr. Carbon related, "was an important dramatic production for the D-E theater department because of the emotional topic and its impact on the culture of our country. Telling the story of Matthew Shepard was an honor and privilege for the cast, crew, and production staff. We all learned more about this young man, homophobia, and the capacity of love in ourselves and others."

In 2009, Mr. Carbon staged the musical *Godspell*, with Jason Goldberg '11, who has already performed several supporting roles at the Metropolitan Opera, in the lead role. "I thoroughly enjoyed playing Jesus," Mr. Goldberg said. "However, the best part of the experience was how Mr. Carbon brought everyone together and we became a family, enabling us to give a truly memorable performance."

In 2014, the vibrant performing arts department, now under the direction of John Littlefield, continues to enrich all members the D-E community. Dwight-Englewood is committed to continuing its rich tradition of theater education and performance to enlighten and bring joy to future generations of performers, stage crews, and audiences.

THE WRITE STUFF

The history of student publications at Dwight School, the Englewood School for Boys, the merged Dwight-Englewood School, and the Bede School is rich and varied. From the 1930s onward, the school's accomplishments in this area have been recognized by one of the nation's oldest and most prominent organizations for student publications, the Columbia Scholastic Press Association (CSPA). Currently, only D-E's literary arts publication, *Calliope*, maintains membership in the association and participates in its yearly competitions, but over the decades, several of our school's publications have been highly honored by the CSPA.

Our school's first known student publication was a handwritten, illustrated paper known as "Woden's Wit and Wisdom," which was read aloud every Wednesday in the Dwight School's assembly. Much more substantial and long-lived was *The Dwightonia*, Dwight School's literary magazine, which first appeared in 1898 and was published continuously until 1949. It grew over those five decades into a preeminent forum for students' essays, short stories, poems, and editorials on issues of school policy and interest. In 1936, *The Dwightonia* was honored by the CSPA with a red ribbon (second place) in that organization's national competition. Along with its main role—featuring student writing—it also served in place of a yearbook from 1917 through 1948, with its June issue being the annual Commencement edition.

In the 1940s, Dwight's Junior School featured an annual magazine called *Let's Pretend*, which contained poems and stories written by girls in the first five grades. Interestingly enough, *Let's*

Pretend sometimes featured short narratives in French, which makes it an early ancestor of the Upper School's foreign language arts/literary magazine, *Parnassus*, which would come along in the 1970s.

In 1949, Dwight School's English department established The Scribblers, an honorary association in which students met to discuss plays and books and to share their own literary works. The Scribblers established a school-wide prose and poetry contest and later an "honor book" that presented outstanding works. In 1958, the literary magazine *Calliope*, which is still published today as a seventy-two-page arts/literary magazine, was founded. In the early 1970s, just preceding the merger that created the Dwight-Englewood School, the Englewood School for Boys had its own creative outlet called, simply, *The Literary Magazine*. A look at its list of contributors for the 1971–72 edition reveals a handful of female names among the boys', signifying the increasing cooperation and crossovers between the two as-yet-separate schools.

Frimi Sagan with students.

Opposite page: In 1940, the *Dwightonia* board meets in Creighton Memorial Library.

The modern era of *Calliope* might be said to have begun in 1973 with the merger of Dwight School and ESB and the beginning of Frimi Sagan's fifteen-year run as the publication's advisor. Gradually, more artwork was included to complement the prose and poetry, establishing for *Calliope* a balanced arts and literary focus that continues to this day and is reflected in other student magazines, such as *Parnassus* (the foreign language literary journal) and *Open Roads* (showcasing Middle School students' work). *Calliope* formally joined the Columbia Scholastic Press Association in the 1970s and has been submitted to that body for judging every year since. In the late 1970s, *Calliope* enjoyed a run of five "First Place" certificates, putting it among the top 5 percent of student magazines submitted. For over three decades, the magazine has frequently earned Gold Medalist status in the CSPA critiques. In fact, *Calliope*'s 2013 issue, the most recent, earned a Gold Medal in the critique, completing a run of nine Gold Medals in the past ten years. Most notably, though, *Calliope* has garnered national recognition by winning three of the coveted and prestigious CSPA "Crown" Awards, including a Gold Crown in 1982; a Silver Crown in 1993 under Ms. Sagan's successors, Nancy Melser and Deborah Minsky; and a Silver Crown in 2011 under current advisor and D-E librarian Steve Petkus.

Parnassus is a foreign language arts and literary magazine similar to *Calliope* in its beautiful layout of text and imagery yet dramatically different in featuring poetry and prose written in almost any language besides English, though sometimes the layout includes an English translation alongside

Calliope covers through the years.

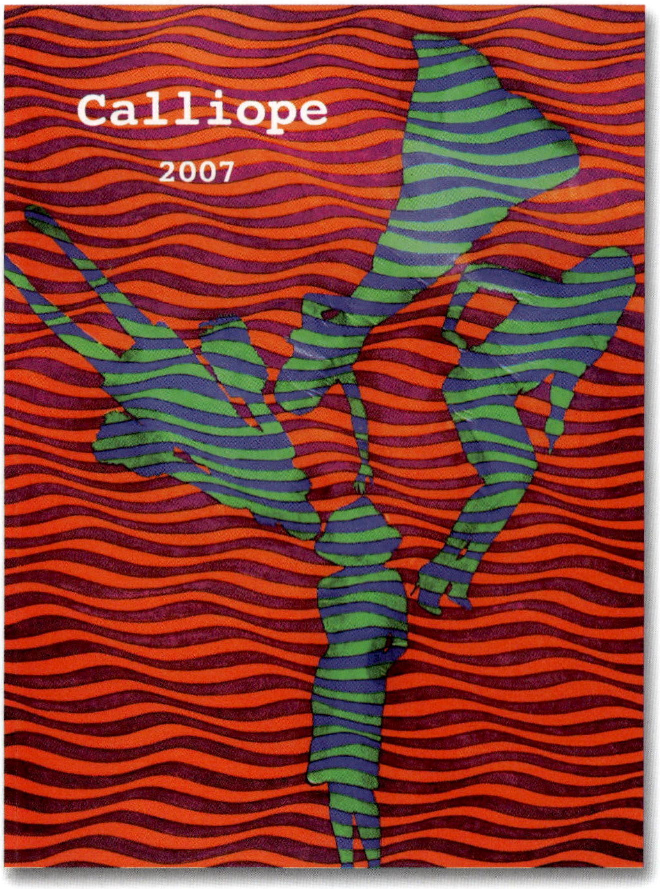

the original. A Dwight School publication known as *Les Polms* dating from the mid-'60s might have been a precursor; in any case, in 1977 *Parnassus* was launched as "a foreign language magazine, comprising poems, short stories, puzzles, artwork, comics, translations from English, or any imaginative contributions from students in German, Latin, Spanish, or French." Over the years, the menu of languages has expanded dramatically to include Russian, Chinese, Hebrew, and Arabic works, among others. *Parnassus* is produced each spring and is lovingly guided by Spanish teacher Abby Kantor, who has been the magazine's advisor since 1983.

The Dwight Junior School's *Let's Pretend*, edited by fifth-graders, was published from 1927 to 1970. *Open Roads*, the Dwight-Englewood Middle School literary and arts magazine, was begun in 1977 and is still going strong today. The spring 1980 issue of *Open Roads* garnered recognition from CSPA: a "First Place" certificate, putting it among the top 5 percent of middle school magazines. *Open Roads* features original art, photography, poetry, and stories by sixth-, seventh-, and eighth-graders.

Guiding the students as advisors today are seventh-grade English teacher Giselle Winters and D-E librarian Carrie Shaurette.

Theatre Fare was established in 1982 as a magazine of the theater department that also served as a playbill. Through the 1980s, students contributed substantial original content, including stories, commentary, and even a production-related crossword puzzle. Since then, *Theatre Fare* has continued to serve as a program for theater productions and a vehicle for commentary by the plays' directors. It is still published today under the guidance of founding advisor and technical director of theater facilities Leon Di Leone.

Student newspapers, of course, have been a staple through the years. At the founding of the Englewood School for Boys in 1928, a student newspaper called *The Spectator* was begun immediately. The title most likely was chosen in emulation of Joseph Addison and Richard Steele's famous London newspaper of 1711–1712. When Marshall Umpleby, who would go on to be the ESB headmaster for thirty years, arrived at the school at the beginning of its second year, he was impressed with the newspaper.

"*The Spectator*," he recalled many years later, a decade after his retirement, "was a monthly publication of attractive make-up, style, and sophisticated content. A few gifted and evidently quite mature upperclassmen under Alfred Everett's direction put out a paper that would do credit to any high school or academy.... There was a good deal of wit and humor, and for the most part a light and deft touch to the writing." *The Spectator* was

The staff of *The Spectator* poses with the tools of their trade in the late 1940s.

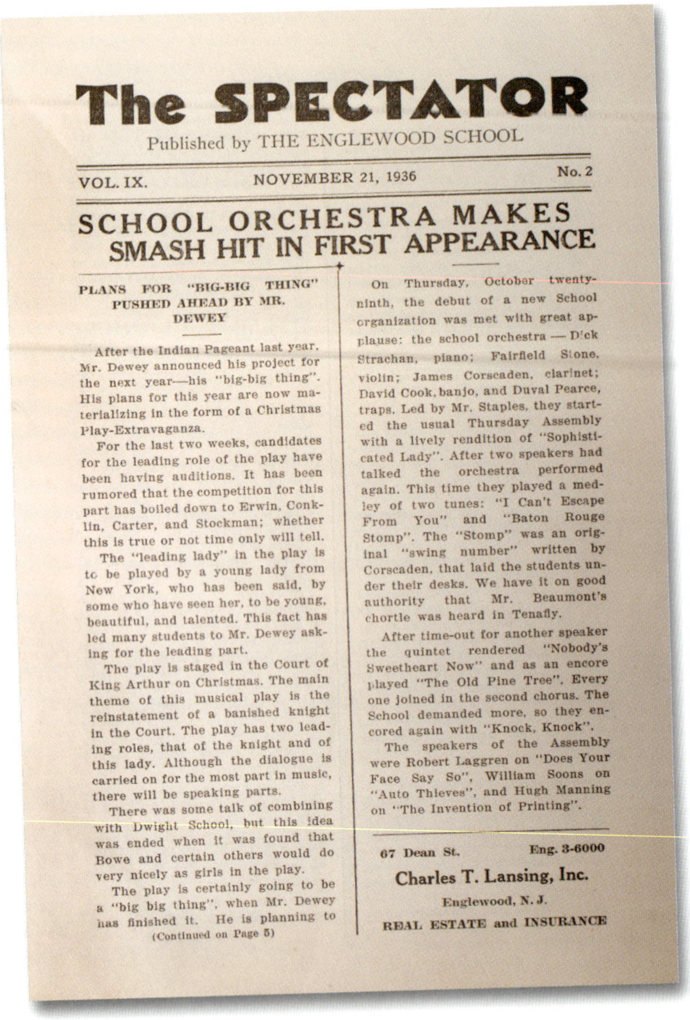

The SPECTATOR

Published by THE ENGLEWOOD SCHOOL

VOL. IX. NOVEMBER 21, 1936 No. 2

SCHOOL ORCHESTRA MAKES SMASH HIT IN FIRST APPEARANCE

PLANS FOR "BIG-BIG THING" PUSHED AHEAD BY MR. DEWEY

After the Indian Pageant last year. Mr. Dewey announced his project for the next year—his "big-big thing". His plans for this year are now materializing in the form of a Christmas Play-Extravaganza.

For the last two weeks, candidates for the leading role of the play have been having auditions. It has been rumored that the competition for this part has boiled down to Erwin, Conklin, Carter, and Stockman; whether this is true or not time only will tell.

The "leading lady" in the play is to be played by a young lady from New York, who has been said, by some who have seen her, to be young, beautiful, and talented. This fact has led many students to Mr. Dewey asking for the leading part.

The play is staged in the Court of King Arthur on Christmas. The main theme of this musical play is the reinstatement of a banished knight in the Court. The play has two leading roles, that of the knight and of this lady. Although the dialogue is carried on for the most part in music, there will be speaking parts.

There was some talk of combining with Dwight School, but this idea was ended when it was found that Bowe and certain others would do very nicely as girls in the play.

The play is certainly going to be a "big big thing", when Mr. Dewey has finished it. He is planning to

(Continued on Page 5)

On Thursday, October twenty-ninth, the debut of a new School organization was met with great applause: the school orchestra — Dick Strachan, piano; Fairfield Stone, violin; James Corscaden, clarinet; David Cook, banjo, and Duval Pearce, traps. Led by Mr. Staples, they started the usual Thursday Assembly with a lively rendition of "Sophisticated Lady". After two speakers had talked the orchestra performed again. This time they played a medley of two tunes: "I Can't Escape From You" and "Baton Rouge Stomp". The "Stomp" was an original "swing number" written by Corscaden, that laid the students under their desks. We have it on good authority that Mr. Beaumont's chortle was heard in Tenafly.

After time-out for another speaker the quintet rendered "Nobody's Sweetheart Now" and as an encore played "The Old Pine Tree". Every one joined in the second chorus. The School demanded more, so they encored again with "Knock, Knock".

The speakers of the Assembly were Robert Laggren on "Does Your Face Say So", William Soons on "Auto Thieves", and Hugh Manning on "The Invention of Printing".

An issue of *The Spectator* from 1936.

published under that title for more than forty years before being incorporated into *Spectrum* in 1970 in anticipation of the merger of the two schools. ESB's Intermediate School also published a regular newspaper called *The Hilltalker* in the mid-1950s. (ESB teams were then nicknamed "Hilltoppers.")

In the 1940s, Dwight School's junior class sponsored a fortnightly "news sheet" called *The Keyhole*. In the spring of 1950, Dwight established a student paper, *The Penton*, and just five years later, the quality of *The Penton* was clear: the paper earned a prestigious "Second Place" certificate from the Columbia Scholastic Press Association in its national competition. In 1965, Dwight School students founded another journalistic publication, *The Forum*, whose aim was "to stimulate thought and controversy within the student body by presenting interesting feature articles and critical analysis of school situations."

In 1970, The Dwight *Forum* and the ESB *Spectator* merged to become *Spectrum* in order to pool funds and writing talent and to produce a better newspaper. Those years also saw ESB's publication of a short-lived editorial paper called *Gorilla*; among the forces behind the "underground" news sheet was Anthony Bourdain '73, celebrity chef and television personality whose tell-all bestseller *Kitchen Confidential: Adventures in the Culinary Underbelly* put him on the map. However, it was *Spectrum* that caught hold and remains the school newspaper to this day. Helmed by advisor and history teacher Peter Bograd since 1995, *Spectrum* produces three or four editions per year "dedicated to the issues, interests, and perspectives of the Dwight-Englewood Upper School."

In the past, *Spectrum* was a member of the Columbia Scholastic Press Association and has garnered some impressive awards for its journalism. It received a "First Place" certificate designation in 1979, 1980, 1988, and 1989, placing it among the top 5 percent of high school student newspapers in the national competition for those years. *Spectrum* also

The *Spectrum* staff is busy with paste-up in the long-gone era of press type.

In the mid-1990s, *Spectrum* editors show off the product of their labors.

achieved Gold Medalist standing in the CSPA critique for its work in 1993 and 1997. The Middle School has occasionally had its own news outlets independent of *Spectrum*. Students published *The Weekly News* in the mid-1980s and *The Dwightee* in the mid-1990s.

The Flea (first published in 2007 and again from 2009 to the present) is a humorous newspaper that features satire and cartoons about Dwight-Englewood life. Visual arts chair Gregg Emery and history teacher Kim Lalli are the paper's current advisors. *The Flea*'s staff also creates and performs a popular assembly-length show, "The Flea Circus," once a year. *Exponent*, D-E's first electronic magazine, began publication in 1994 under Peter Davies, then director of technology. Since the Internet was still in a fledgling state, it came formatted on PC-compatible disks and featured "animation and other graphics that couldn't be seen in a two-dimensional publication." Billed as "The Math, Science, and Technology Magazine of Dwight-Englewood School," *Exponent* became an online-only magazine through D-E's internal web page and was published there into the new century.

Although it was neither by nor for students, a survey of publications at D-E would be incomplete without a mention of *Graham House Review*, a good indicator of the lively creative life at the school at the time.

"In the winter of 1975," co-founder Peter Balakian '69 recalled, "Bruce Smith and I decided to start our own poetry journal and named it after the post-Civil War stone mansion at 81 Lincoln Street that was owned by D-E and in which I had a two-room garret on the third floor. We felt the house was stone-solid and wanted our magazine to be as well." The magazine would feature poets from all over, many of them firmly established. Both Balakian and Smith are Bucknell graduates, were teaching at D-E then, and are now widely published poets. "Our first issue came out in the spring of 1976 and featured some marvelous poets including Richard Hugo, James Tate, Gary Soto, Albert Goldbarth, and many young poets. We published the magazine for the next twenty years, taking it with us wherever we went."

Of all student publications, yearbooks are the likeliest to linger on bookshelves or in attics. Dwight School's first yearbook, *The Record*, appeared from 1908 until the United States entered World War I in 1917. To save costs, the Class of 1917 chose to bind its yearbook in paper instead of leather and donate the savings to the United States war effort. Then, from 1917 until 1948, the June issue of the school's literary magazine, *The Dwightonia*, played the role of commemorating graduation and graduates that more typically fell to a yearbook. *The Blue and White*, the Englewood School for Boys yearbook, was first published in 1941 and continued until the merger in 1973. Dwight-Englewood's yearbook, *Carpe Diem*, was established then and continues under the leadership of photography/videography teacher John McCabe, who has been the yearbook advisor since 1992.

ARS LONGA

"'Learn math, mechanics, electricity, navigation and meteorology. There is no time for poetry and the arts.' This is a doctrine which schools must combat," long-time Englewood School for Boys headmaster Marshall Umpleby wrote in reaction to the pressures for change that resulted from World War II. Though this debate, about the value of a liberal arts education versus a more practical (and potentially lucrative) one, remains lively today and drives curriculum changes, Dwight-Englewood School and its predecessors have always valued the arts—visual arts and music—and featured them in their curricula.

The visual arts at D-E have benefited from a commitment to individual expression and continue to thrive today. In the early years at ESB, long before the merger, the arts program was divided into fine and manual arts. The ESB fine arts department incorporated watercolors, oils, charcoal, crayons, pencil sketching, woodcarving, and sculpting, while the manual arts department offered boys the chance to develop manual skills, especially in woodworking. In the early '70s, under the direction of Robert Barsamian, the fine arts department at ESB and then Dwight-Englewood came into its own.

"We took over the old wooden two-story building and created a home for the fine arts," Mr. Barsamian remembered. "We had exchange programs with the schools in New York City and art openings in our great gallery space for exhibitions by both professional artists and students." With a staff that included Cornel Ferat, Nicholas Barberi, and Alix Euwer, the department offered courses in ceramics, sculpting,

When Umpleby Hall opened in 1965, it freed up what had been ESB's main classroom building to be devoted to the visual arts.

Opposite page: This art studio was built in 1933 in the loft of the first ESB property at 35 Dwight Place. Fifth- and sixth-grade boys are at work here.

This Dwight art class is at work on portraiture. The model, perhaps a member of the class, sits with arms crossed at center.

This Dwight arts room on the second floor of Hulst House was badly damaged by fire in 1966 but restored.

photography, and movie making. Albert Greco and Tom Wilcox taught a cinema course, which was wildly popular with students and gave rise to a film festival. Arts department chair Lenore Berck, with the help of Madeline Cosman, a parent, created a Medieval Festival that combined the talents of students and faculty members of the arts department.

At Dwight, after a fire in the art room in 1966, visual arts facilities moved from rooms shared with other disciplines to single-use studio spaces, dedicated to making art.

The transformation of the Dwight School gym into the Swartley Arts Center in November 1982 completed the picture. A major gift from Mrs. John C. Swartley coupled with the donations it sparked provided a new, efficient arts facility for use by D-E students and faculty. This array of studios, classrooms, galleries, and offices honors John Swartley, president for many years of the Three School Development Foundation.

Arts courses and related clubs have regularly been added to the curricular and co-curricular offerings, targeting students' specific interests as well as technological advancements in art production. In 1952, a Photography Club was formed at Dwight, dedicated to improving members' camera techniques, and a new darkroom enabled students to polish their work.

Later, there was a photography course at D-E. Architecture was introduced as a course in 1991 in response to student demand. In 1987, a program called Creative Visions thrived as an addition to the regular curriculum where alumni and members of the community came to campus to talk with students about their career in the arts.

In 2003, D-E initiated the Community Arts Network, linking established local artists to the school's curriculum while providing a visual arts forum for Englewood. Visual arts have become integrated into other academic disciplines. The Middle School's Grade 6 Identity Unit includes self-portraits in tandem with monologues on personal identity, including ethnicity, religion, sports, and hobbies. At the twice-annual Arts Festival, which includes performances by the school's vocal and instrumental ensembles, student art is exhibited throughout the Klein Campus Center. Art on display ranges from ceramics and silk screenings to oil paintings, pencil drawings, and mixed media works.

The visual arts department exposes students to both classic and contemporary masterpieces through off-campus field trips and gallery visits, while bringing alumni artists to campus for seminars and exhibits. Beyond an annual "Senior Spotlight Exhibit," which features the work of graduating students, the visual arts department coordinates students' entries into the national competition for Scholastic Art & Writing Awards. Additionally, students are regularly featured in local, New York City, and tri-state-area exhibits and galleries. In 2014, the visual arts department initiated a professional artist-in-residence program that culminated in a collaborative exhibit.

The annual Puppet Parade, a tradition of nearly fifteen years' standing, entails the creation of a menagerie of puppet animals by all Lower School students, who then march together across campus to the delight of Middle and Upper School faculty and students. Middle and Upper School students pair up with Lower School children to create such cooperative projects as "Kindergarten Zoo."

And then there's music. From entirely original operas created by fifth-graders to the enduring legacy of a handbell choir, from the rock-and-roll of Jazz Rock to the inception of resident ensembles that showcase faculty members' extraordinary talents—here and elsewhere a vigorous and sustained tradition of excellence runs through the history of the Music Department at Dwight-Englewood School. Right from the first, music played an important role in a Dwight School education. Early catalogues and brochures list faculty members with impressive credentials. The teacher of vocal music during the year the school opened, Madame F. Roena Medini, is described as a "pupil of Lamperti, Vannuceini, and Salvi, for six years Prima Donna in Italian Opera."

At Dwight there was the Glee Club, and then the Choral Club was established in 1938 and the Choir a few years later. "Dwight School recognizes

The Glee Club, seen here with various stringed instruments, was Dwight's earliest vocal ensemble.

Joe Erwin, here at center with the nine members of Choir, the elite vocal group, was the focal point of music at Dwight for decades. His wife, Kathleen, holds Geoffrey Bear, the long-revered senior class mascot.

the ever increasing role of music in the cultural life of America," the 1930 Course of Study notes, "and pays tribute to it by giving music an important part in the life of the school."

Helene Williams, in charge of Dwight's music program from 1943 to 1954, wrote that "the main object of the Music Department is to enrich the life of the students not only for the present but also for the future.... While some strict adherence to rules is necessary, encouragement is nevertheless given to free uninhibited creative activity."

But for generations of Dwight girls, music meant Joseph Erwin.

"Mr. Erwin came to Dwight as an accompanist for the Choral Club and piano teacher for the boarding students in 1948," according to the Spring 1972 Dwight *Alumnae Bulletin*. "In 1954 he became the Director of the Music Department, where he developed a fine curriculum, and an image to some as a friend more than a teacher. One of Mr. Erwin's efforts particularly well known and loved by us all," the article went on, "is the Christmas Pageant, which is performed jointly with the Drama Department. Here he blends handbells and voices which, together with the tableaux, create an atmosphere where the peace and joy of the holiday season must be felt." (In fact, the Pageant in its original form would survive just three more years.)

A highlight for the Choral Club was its annual collaboration with the Yale Freshman

Yale freshmen and the Dwight Choral Club pose at their joint concert in 1948.

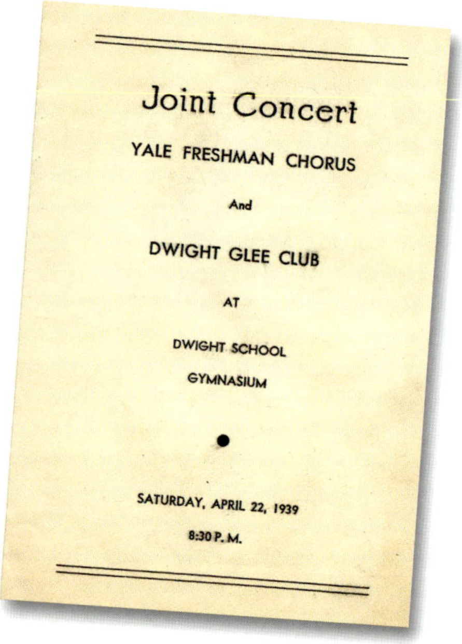

Joint Concert

YALE FRESHMAN CHORUS

And

DWIGHT GLEE CLUB

AT

DWIGHT SCHOOL

GYMNASIUM

•

SATURDAY, APRIL 22, 1939

8:30 P. M.

In 1939, the third year of the joint concert, the Dwight group was the Glee Club, led by Margaret Nikoloric. The program included Bach, Brahms, and Handel, some folk songs, and ended with the Yale and Dwight alma maters.

Glee Club in a spring concert, a tradition that began in 1937 and continued, with a brief interruption during World War II, until 1964. "Boola-boola! Rah! Rah! Bulldog! And feminine hearts went plop as Yale descended in our midst," according to *The Dwightonia*. Typically held at the Roosevelt School in Englewood, the concerts featured works by Mozart, Bach, Grieg, Schubert, and others. Begun in 1941, these concerts continued through 1968. Often the concert was followed by a dance, to which the Yale men were invited. Often there was a dinner after the rehearsal and before the performance. Bev Holmes Prevost '62 remembers gathering at the home of classmate Kathe Foote Lingamfelter '62 after the performance "where we sang even more, all the Yale songs, and then the gals had a sleepover. Starting in sixth and seventh grade," she said, "Dwight introduced me to my lifelong love of singing parts, and I'm still singing alto in the church choir."

The concert and the Christmas Pageant were the two major performances of the Dwight Choral Club, but the Choral Club and Choir also participated in a variety of concerts in collaboration with other schools, including Hackley, Horace Mann, Elisabeth Morrow, and Dwight Morrow. These concerts, all under the direction of Mr. Erwin, included a performance on CBS Radio in December 1962. The Choral Club also sang in chapel in the fall and at the Father-Daughter Dinner in the spring.

For a time the club also had an annual concert with Choate School in mid-May, and a highlight occurred when the singers received an invitation to record Bach's Mass in G Minor with Choate for broadcast by a New Haven television station. "The most able members of the Choral Club are chosen to sing in Choir, a group of 20 girls or one third of the Choral Club," according to a presentation at "The Dwight That Is" in May 1964. "Although this group sings together with Choral Club in all the latter's concerts, Choir performs several songs independent of the larger group. Choir was once again honored this year by an invitation to record Christmas music for the CBS Radio Network."

At both Dwight and ESB, students were taught to appreciate as well as perform music. Dwight had a box at the Metropolitan Opera from 1909 until 1970, taking them from the "old" Met to the new one at Lincoln Center. Boys from ESB were often invited to attend the opera performances, which were typically Saturday matinees.

Albert Metzger, long-time history teacher at ESB, directed the Music Appreciation Club in which all seventy-two Lower schoolboys participated. The object was to teach the boys to listen to music intelligently and to "broaden each student's outlook on music, by presenting the less familiar composers and their compositions, their styles and influences upon other composers," Mr. Metzger noted. "There were issues with this club in the form of attendance and a poorly functioning Victrola."

Dwight also had a handbell choir, begun in 1955 by Mr. Erwin, who was responsible for bringing the bells from the Whitechapel Foundry in England and creating special arrangements for the ringers. The handbells were a gift from Mrs. Williams in memory of Mrs. Hulst, a former principal. Mr. Erwin traveled over the summer of 1956 to Buffalo, where he spent a week with an established handbell group learning the techniques of ringing the bells and arranging music, as there was none published for handbells at the time. After arranging a piece for the bells, Mr. Erwin taught a group of faculty to play and, with their performance, ceremonially gave the bells to the students. Mr. Erwin arranged a number of scores including sacred hymns and carols for Christmas and Easter, as well as many secular folk songs. Enthusiasm for the Bell Choir was apparent when fifty girls signed up to audition.

Featured at Christmas concerts and other events, handbells became a fixture at the school and remain so today. This popularity led to regular

The handbell choir became so popular at Dwight and later D-E that the program grew to include multiple ensembles.

concert tours, not just locally but also regionally and even internationally. In 1975, a group of twenty-four Choral Club and Bell Choir members traveled to Romania on a three-week tour that covered most of the country. The trip was at the invitation of the Romanian government, and the students were expected to give at least three concerts a week.

"While in Romania, the students were given wide exposure to youth centers and worker housing," according the Fall 1997 issue of *D-E Today*, and censorship of some of their religious texts caused some consternation, though the students were still "able to reflect on the spiritual experiences they had with the Romanian people." As the handbell program's popularity continued to grow, Dwight-Englewood in the 1980s acquired a second set of bells, United States-made by Schulmerich, to be used by Middle School students.

The Choral Club, Choir, and Bell Choir were designed, according to Mr. Erwin, to "develop music reading skills, positive attitudes in group activity and, most importantly, a deepening awareness and sensitivity to the less visible nature of the human being, which becomes more visible as the students perform compositions of some of the world's most perceptive persons."

Music was also important to Dwight Junior School students. In the mid-1930s, they focused mainly on melody, rhythm, and harmony in their music studies, while fifth- and sixth-graders focused on three important chords of music and the playing of simple melodies, in addition to sight-singing and music appreciation. The Junior School's music curriculum included Instrumental Music, Choral Class, and Vocal Performance. Choral Class provided students at Dwight School with an appreciation for composers ranging from Beethoven and Mendelssohn to Brahms and Rubinstein.

Another outstanding area of the music program, the Dwight-Englewood Orchestra, which includes both faculty and students, made its debut on the Lillian Pitkin Schenck Auditorium stage in 1975. (Before that, the orchestra had been a composite ensemble of instrumentalists from Dwight, Englewood School for Boys, and Elisabeth Morrow School.) That year, the orchestra was chosen as one of the select American groups to participate in the Romanian tour, along with the Bell Choir and Choral Club. The orchestra has continued to be an integral component of the school program, recently touring both locally and globally, including joint performances with such ensembles as the Spence School Orchestra and trips to Great Britain and Central Europe in June 2011 and June 2013.

Ensembles featuring faculty musicians also have been showcased. Dr. Rodney De Jarnett initiated a Head of School Series in 2010 that featured exceptional professionals in the performing arts, many of whom teach D-E students or direct student musical groups. Concerts featuring the resident ensembles 315 East (a chamber group) and Jazz Vistas performed memorable concerts that included "From Vienna to Prague" (with works by Mozart and Dvořák) and "From Boogaloo to The Beatles."

Two of the biggest draws in the Upper School are Jazz Rock and Stage Band, both of which began during Lenore Berck's tenure as arts chair. Jazz Rock was founded in 1977 by Byron Conner as a group of ten vocalists. "Students must understand that they can play anything," according to Rob DeBellis, who took over the group in 1986, by which time the instrumental component had become more central. "They should put forth a more personal statement instead of just working to play popular music to please the audience." Today Jazz Rock remains an integral part of the school's music program and offers a standing-room-only Upper School assembly performance on the day prior to the Winter Break each year. D-E alumni such as The Paper Dolls' Chip Thomas '99 and Shinobi Ninja's Dave Machinist '01 and Mike Machinist '01, all successful and popular performers, attribute their success and inspiration to their early Jazz Rock years on the Schenck and then Hajjar Auditorium stages.

StringJam on the occasion of its Carnegie Hall concert in 2014.

In 2011, Jazz Rock celebrated its twenty-fifth year under Mr. DeBellis's leadership with an outdoor reunion "Jam" on Leggett Field, which featured a lineup of Jazz Rock alumni. With songs from "I Love Rock & Roll" to "We Are Family," Jazz Rock's reunion was "both a live and love rock fest," in the words of a returning performer.

Stage Band, begun in 1987 under the direction of Ann Crawford, focused primarily on jazz standards. In 1995, after Mr. DeBellis had taken charge, its concert was moved from the auditorium to the cafeteria, thus becoming more a cabaret than a concert. String, reed, and percussion-specific ensembles have important presences as well. For instance, StringJam, composed of Upper School students and founded in 2005 by violin teacher Annaliesa Place, is a highly selective ensemble of approximately

The Annual Winter Arts Festival continues to be a popular event for the community.

twenty. The group regularly performs on tours both locally and regionally and also participates in music outreach programs designed to engage younger "stringers," including a performance in 2011 with the Suzuki Strings Ensemble at the National Presbyterian Church in Washington, D.C. StringJam achieved another milestone in February 2014 with its Carnegie Hall debut, at which alumna violinist Harumi Rhodes '97 was also featured.

Vocal ensembles have been a consistent presence at the school, both prior to and since the 1973 merger. Dwight had its prestigious Choral Club and Choir. At ESB—in 1967, for example—students were encouraged to participate in at least one aspect of the music program, which included such regular classes as music theory. ESB's Upper School Glee Club sang at assemblies, and these older boys joined Lower School students in annual concerts.

Today, new music courses continue to be integrated into the performing arts curriculum. Middle and Upper School music teacher Matt Schukis created an a cappella group called the Dwight Mix. This group was a huge success and grew to be so popular that additional a cappella groups were developed, including Mr. Schukis's The Treble Makers, a group of twelve girls. African Drumming and Show Choir have also become new Discovery Classes, which function outside the standard curriculum. A Guitar Ensemble course has attracted both acoustic and electric players.

The fifth-grade opera.

Unique musical opportunities abound across all three divisions at the school. Of particular note is the Lower School's Creating Original Opera Program for children in Grade 5, created at Bede in 1986. The program was initiated and is directed by Lower School music teacher Mary Heveran, who is also a member of the New York Metropolitan Opera's Educational Department's board of trustees. From there she brought the concept, which has students managing the entire production, including determining theme and plot, writing the script, music, and lyrics, building the sets, devising costumes and makeup, orchestrating the sound, working the lights, and managing public relations—as well as performing.

As it long has been, today the hill is alive with the sounds of music—jazz, classical, bells, vocal, made by students of all ages and faculty as well.

FIELDS OF DREAMS

At both Dwight School and the Englewood School for Boys, athletics played a major role in the lives of students from the beginning, and that surely remains the case at Dwight-Englewood. In the early years at Dwight, horseback riding, tennis, "basket-ball" (as it was then spelled), and softball were the major sports. The girls first played basketball in 1906, just fifteen years after James Naismith invented the game.

"Greater activity has been shown in athletics this year than ever before," according to the December 1902 *Dwightonia*, the student magazine. "The new gymnasium had a great deal to do with this of course. For several years now we have been hoping that we might have one, and now that it is here we are supporting it heartily. So far, most of the work has been class work, but a little bar work is done and we feel quite confident that we shall all become acrobats by June."

"As we do not believe in being left behind [by] any fad, especially a good one, we devote one morning a week to fencing under the direction of Col. Schultz," *The Dwightonia* reported on another occasion. "But of all the forms of exercise basket-ball is still the favorite. Every afternoon the field is in use. There are now three teams and their substitutes. With so many girls playing, enthusiasm is not lacking, and spirited games are in good progress every day." Each May came Senior Field Day, with races, high jump, long jump, and ball throws. Seniors competed against the freshmen, sophomores, and juniors.

Originally, competition was intramural—in 1909 an intramural tennis tournament was held for the first time, though Dwight girls had played

Basketball was an important sport at Dwight from the early years. This 1926 varsity team was undefeated.

Opposite page: The Dwight Riding Club in the early years of the twentieth century. In the background is Graham House, purchased in 1968 by the Three School Development Foundation.

Field hockey in 1938 on what would be called Leggett Field. In the background is the new Englewood School campus at 363 East Palisade Avenue.

Dwight archers in the 1930s.

the game since the 1890s—but, as the June 1911 *Dwightonia* reported, "On Saturday March 18th, the basket-ball team played a game with Rosemary Hall, of Greenwich, Connecticut, in their gymnasium, with Rosemary winning by a score of 28-11.... The Senior Class basket-ball team played the Junior Class team in the gymnasium on Friday, March 24th. The game score was 9-6 in favor of the Juniors." But Dwight beat Horace Mann 18 to 12 in 1911, and from 1914 through 1917 the team was undefeated.

In 1927, former all-American Linda Styer introduced field hockey to Dwight, played on the First Presbyterian Church field until Leggett Field was completed in 1931, and by the 1950s the girls were playing paddle tennis, and interscholastic sports included field hockey in the fall, basketball in the winter, and tennis and lacrosse in the spring. Fencing became a competitive sport and a requirement. As a part of the physical education program, students could participate in archery, tennis, volleyball, gymnastics, and yoga. Horseback riding at the Pegasus Riding Stable in Rockleigh was an after-school option. In the early years of the school there was a Tramping Club.

Baseball at Dwight in the late 1940s.

An even wider array of sports was offered by the 1960s, including dancing, badminton, and baseball. There were new showers and locker rooms in the gym and a full-sized hockey field, double all-weather tennis courts, and paddle tennis courts. Sports were managed through the Athletic Association and the head of the physical education department.

By the late 1940s, Dwight had an Athletic Association to "organize and fulfill all the activities of the Athletic Department and keep it running smoothly…. Among other things, the A.A. has tried to promote school spirit by encouraging spectators to attend the various games played both outside and within the school, throughout the year." Every girl was a member of the Athletic Association and assigned to either a yellow or white team.

"She always had time to talk to students," recalled Peggy Bloch Schneider '68 of Jeanne Phelps, who was Dwight's director of physical education after Ruth Earle Brittan '34. "Phelpsie," as her friends called her, took that role in 1963 and served Dwight until the 1973 merger, remaining at D-E until 1981. "The Dwight Physical Education

"There is lots of enthusiasm over the tennis tournament this year. No doubt it is our new extra special 50th Anniversary Fund tennis courts…." *The Dwightonia*, June 1939.

Dwight's paddle-tennis courts, in use here circa 1950, occupied the space where Silberfein Gym now stands.

Department," she wrote, "feels that we have a unique opportunity in helping girls develop and mature during their years at Dwight, providing learning experiences in both the physical and social dimensions of sport. We feel that developing those intangibles i.e. good sportsmanship, self discipline and responsibility for self and others, is as important as becoming skilled in both team and individual activities.... We are primarily physical educators," she continued, "who recognize the values of competition for girls who wish to become more skilled in a given activity, and who enjoy competing against other schools, whether in team or individual activities."

Right from the beginning sports were important at the Englewood School for Boys, though small student numbers were a limiting factor at first. "In the Senior School was a fairly husky football squad coached by Butler Beaumont," long-time ESB headmaster Marshall Umpleby wrote decades later, recalling the situation in 1929 at the year-old school when he arrived. "Several games were played that year with second and JV teams of neighboring high schools. I can still see Patrick Henry Davis, Jr. '32 running back kicks or dashes from scrimmage the length of the Presbyterian Church field, which may have been a dozen yards short of a regulation gridiron." Football teams in the early years numbered just twelve to fifteen players.

The 1930 ESB football squad was undermanned but scrappy. Jack-of-all-trades Butler Beaumont was the coach.

"The Englewood School for Boys played a game with Boy Scout Troop 26 on October 19," according to the November 1928 issue of *The Spectator*, the student newspaper, reporting on a game in the school's first fall. "The Scouts were heavier, but otherwise the teams were evenly matched. The Scouts kicked off and Embree of the school ran back for almost 15 yards before he was tackled. The school played well up to the third quarter, when they fumbled the ball, losing to Troop 26... with a final score of 6-0." The December issue noted that "in the final game of the season... against our old rival, Troop 26, the school played its best game of the year.... Mr. Beaumont has been taking motion pictures of the football team in action at practice. In this manner the mistakes are easily evident.... Here is an innovation in school athletics."

In December of 1929, Mr. Umpleby established a boys' ice hockey team. The December 1929 *Spectator* notes: "Under the direction of Mr. Umpleby and Mr. Hall [ESB's second and first headmasters] the School's hockey team is slowly being whipped into shape.... We anticipate a winning team and a good season." Baseball had been established the previous spring, with games played at the Englewood Field Club, which was also where the hockey team skated.

In 1930, ESB's first varsity basketball team won its opening game 28 to 21. "Mr. Umpleby," *The Spectator* reported, "has been doing his level best to teach those who come out for the team how to get the best out of the game without letting it become too boring to them. All that is needed now is a stronger spirit of cooperation." The first of what was to become an annual sports dinner had been held the previous June. Fathers, trustees, students, and faculty were invited. The A.C. Dent Sportsmanship Medal was awarded and the "athletic numerals for the year" given out by Mr. Beaumont.

The coach of the 1937-38 varsity basketball team was Arthur Umpleby, at left, brother of Marshall, the headmaster. The Umps and Dux Trophy, established in 1935 and awarded to an outstanding sophomore athlete who displays sportsmanlike qualities, honors Marshall and Arthur—and Butler Beaumont, whose nickname was "Dux," Latin for leader.

Luke Ward came to ESB in September 1934 and spent twenty-five years as athletic director and coach. Some say that he single-handedly changed sports at ESB.

"Football was Luke's middle name," according to Mr. Umpleby—a perhaps unsurprising proclivity, since he was born in Alabama and graduated from Auburn. Englewood School's small size limited its competitiveness in sports at first and games were often intramural, with only limited competition against outside teams, but that would change.

"Mr. Ward saw prospects of developing a real football team" in 1936, Mr. Umpleby recalled,

The 1942 ESB varsity baseball team. Coach Luke Ward, the mainstay of Boys' School athletics for decades, is at left.

"and sought opponents among the independent schools of New York." In fact, the 1937 team would be not only undefeated but also untied and un-scored-upon.

"I know that D's and F's are not popular letters there at the school," Mr. Ward wrote years later. "In our program they were. Desire–Dedication–Discipline!!! Fairness–Fortitude–Faith!!!" He felt that his mandate when he had been hired was "to aid in the promotion and maintenance of discipline, which had become a shambles during the Depression." When he returned to ESB in 1946 after a stint in the military, a handful of sturdy GIs also arrived to prepare for college and became the foundation for another championship football team, with undefeated seasons in 1946 and 1947. Mr. Ward also coached baseball. By the time he retired from ESB in 1959 amidst a fanfare of accolades, Luke Ward had become known as the dean of Bergen County coaches. He loved Englewood School and the school loved him.

While Dwight got its gymnasium in 1902 and the field now known as Leggett in 1931, for nearly three decades Englewood School's athletes were migrants and their "fields of dreams" various: borrowed, leased, sometimes distant, and often unsatisfactory. When the school was located at 35 Dwight Place, boys used without charge the field and gymnasium of the adjacent First Presbyterian Church. (The school benefited in various ways from close relations with the church). They played baseball and hockey at the Englewood

Field Club. With the move in 1937 to 363 East Palisade Avenue, ESB had its own gym for the first time: a small one, constructed from a moveable building that came with the school from Dwight Place. Next to the Dwight field was a sloping

ESB basketball in the school's early years was played on the First Presbyterian court.

ESB baseball in 1936 was played on the Englewood Field Club diamond. The ump is "Ump"—Headmaster Marshall Umpleby—and the batter George Shultz '38, who would become the United States Secretary of State.

apple orchard that in 1940 would be graded into a football field, albeit a slightly undersized one.

The mid-1950s brought big breakthroughs: in 1954 with the dedication of the first portion of the Upper Field on North Woodland Street in Englewood Cliffs (rededicated a decade later as Solomon Field) and in 1955 with the opening of the "Auxiliary Building" with a first-class gymnasium. Both are still in use today. The North Woodland property had been sold to the school in 1946 at cost by Nathan Solomon, an ESB parent. Under the direction of J. Wright Taussig, Jr. '42 a long-time ESB trustee, it was, according to the *New York Times*, transformed from "6 1/2 acres of swamp and woodlands into what could eventually be one of the finest athletic fields in Northern New Jersey." The process took years. Fill came from the blasting for the lower level of the George Washington Bridge. Luke Ward claimed to have added to the mix soil from all the fifty states, collected from friends all over the country with the help of ESB parents and teachers. In 1968, the Upper Field was renamed Solomon Field.

The sports teams themselves at ESB, always called "the Hilltoppers," were renamed at roughly the same time in the wake of widespread student sentiment for a change. In a landslide, students voted for "Bulldogs" over such choices as Vikings and Falcons, and that remains the name of all sports teams at Dwight-Englewood School. A catalyst for the renaming was Carlos Henriquez, whom Mr. Umpleby called "the athletic director I've been seeking" in 1963 when he appointed him. He coached track, cross-country, and wrestling during his decade at ESB, and also raised championship bulldogs and touted their virtues: courage and loyalty. Henriquez's international champion bulldog Lucky Ace II became the school's flesh-and-blood mascot and appeared at all the games.

Carlos Henriquez's prizewinning bulldog, Lucky Ace II.

Through the generosity of Sam Davis '70 and his family, D-E now has a 900-pound, seven-foot-long bulldog on the patio between Pope Science Hall and the Khubani Center for Performing Arts. Created by Branly Cadet, a noted sculptor, the bulldog traveled more than 3,000 miles by truck from the Artworks Foundry in Berkley, California. Davis encourages students to touch the bulldog's paw for luck.

The spring of 1960 had brought some bad news for the ESB football program with the surprise announcement that varsity football had been suspended for lack of participants. But before long the sport would come back in a major way, culminating in an unblemished record in 1968.

"Everything about an undefeated season is about growth and commitment, about desire and discipline," team co-captain Peter Balakian '69 recalled in 1999 when he was inducted into the school's Athletic Hall of Fame (a recognition

Sam Davis '70, who with his family provided the funds for this bulldog statue, gives a thumbs-up at its dedication. Head of School Dr. Rodney De Jarnett holds the microphone.

initiated in 1996 that now honors seventy-two athletes and nine distinguished teams). "Everything is about a team seeing how far it can push itself, about what's beyond its grasp—that's what desire is." Mr. Balakian, a nationally known poet, memoirist, and Armenian Holocaust scholar, continued: "My coaches were among my best teachers—and I had many superb academic teachers." And not only the football team prospered in the mid-1960s. From 1963 to 1966, the wrestling team won twenty-six out of twenty-seven meets and in 1967 and 1968 were state champions. The soccer team was undefeated in 1964, 1965, and 1966. Englewood School teams were state champions in varsity football, varsity soccer, and varsity cross-country in the mid-'60s.

Post-merger, the athletic department continued to offer a large selection of sports along with a comprehensive physical education program. Since most often teachers also act as coaches at D-E, students develop relationships with teachers outside of the classroom. "Being on a team is not a convenient commitment," Tom Curry, athletic director from 1991 to 2008, said. "It is about learning about persistence, dedication, and drive. Goals are nothing without action, and the first part of any action in any organization is to be there."

The rifle team at ESB had long been popular with the boys, but after the merger it became coeducational, if only in a limited way, attracting the attention of Diana Dallas '74, who became the first and only girl on the team and earned the Sharpshooter Bar 4 standing. The rifle range, under the ESB activities building, was finally dismantled in 2010, though the team had disbanded back in 1983.

Upper School girls' volleyball was introduced as a new sport in 2004 and had its first match in November; Middle School teams followed. Weight training and conditioning had become a part of the program in 1998 when the school opened a new facility with machines and free weights. Among the notable D-E teams were 1978 and 1991 boys' soccer, 1980 girls' tennis, 1999 and 1992 boys' tennis, and 2002 boys' basketball.

"The physical education program at Dwight-Englewood is large and complex," according to Chris Schmid, chair of Physical Education and Health from 1977 to 2009. "The program exists in two distinct areas: physical education classes and interscholastic teams. In its entirety, the program is an integral part of the educational experience offered by the School." That remains true today.

Dwight Junior School athletics were intramural, white versus yellow, the school's colors. This is the 1957 White Team.

Tennis continues to be a smashing sport at D-E!

Today, the Athletic Hall of Fame highlights the schools' tradition of athletic excellence and honors "those individuals who have achieved a high level of success during their careers as student athletes, coaches or through other significant contributions to the school's athletic program. Its purpose," its mission statement continues, "is to perpetuate the memory of those who have brought distinction, honor and excellence to the Dwight School, Englewood School for Boys and the Dwight-Englewood School." Inductees are honored each year during Alumni Reunion Weekend, giving the school community the occasion to recall athletic successes and dreams realized.

Placing the tag.

HELPING OTHERS

Right from the beginning, Dwight School actively encouraged service to the community, both locally and nationally, but at first there was no formal community service organization. Whenever a worthy cause came to the attention of Frances Leggett '96 and Maud Jackson Hulst '94, co-principals for decades, they appointed a "Chairman of Charities" to collect funds. After 1933, however, with the coming of the Depression and then World War II, so many requests were made for assistance that a more formal, ongoing structure replaced the ad hoc arrangement.

"Then there is the Service League," Miss Leggett said in 1947, "under which comes the Red Cross and the Northfield League, which are both interested in doing for others at home or abroad." In 1950, the Dwight student body voted to combine the Northfield League (the Dwight chapter of this religion-based organization was established in 1934) and the Service League (including the Red Cross) into one group called the Dwight Service Organization, with Marjorie Cannon Bailey '17 as faculty advisor until she retired in 1963. DSO provided the opportunity by which "a girl could contribute in service instead of (just) money," according to Mrs. Bailey, and therefore "service was a finer gift by which a girl could cancel her debt to society." The DSO was imbued with her philosophy.

The goal of DSO, according to a 1952 *Alumnae Bulletin*, was "to serve God and man. This organization contributes a great deal to the life at Dwight and is held in high esteem." And from a 1962 *Bulletin*: "The DSO gives every girl the opportunity to serve others in the community, nation and world. Therefore, the chief aim of this

Opposite page: Travel to Ecuador as part of the Summer 2013 World Challenge (which combines international travel, service, and student leadership) is among the most recent examples of community outreach at D-E.

organization is to develop girls who care about people and their needs."

By the early 1960s, DSO included several branches: the Service League, with the chairman of volunteers responsible for sending volunteers from Dwight to Englewood Hospital and Memorial House (which provided services to children and the elderly in the Englewood community); the Red Cross; the Children's Theater, with students presenting well-known children's stories on Saturday afternoons (proceeds going to a Service Organization fund that was distributed to various charities); the Northfield League; the Foster Parent Plan, supporting underprivileged children in Europe; and American Field Service, a cultural exchange program.

The Northfield League, the religious branch of DSO, held conferences each June to bring together "outstanding Christian leaders and students for a week of study, discussion, and worship." In 1947, Dwight School sponsored a Northfield Conference on its campus, where, according to a local newspaper account, "the young women discussed the belief in religious and social welfare programs in the schools, and that the future depends on a deeper understanding among young and old about the life and ways of other peoples."

"DSO has, by real participation, not by talk alone, involved Dwight girls in the problems of the world, and in some of their possible alleviation or solution," wrote Janet Peterson, faculty advisor of DSO, in the fall of 1968 about a Peace Corps School in India that DSO helped to build. Earlier that year DSO had supported a carnival to raise funds for a two-room elementary school in Madras, India. DSO also sponsored foster children; the 1969 DSO publication *Getting it Together* included a thank-you letter from a South Vietnamese first-grader named Mai Thi Hue. During the Vietnam War DSO also sponsored a thirteen-year-old boy named Dao van Hiep. "He is grateful to his foster parents and hopes to become a school teacher one day," wrote his caseworker in Vietnam.

As the Dwight-Englewood merger approached, DSO was made up of the entire student body of Dwight and ESB. In 1970, the organization sponsored a Halloween party for the Leonard Johnson Daycare Center, with dozens of students from both Dwight and ESB supervising the children in the school cafeteria. An additional service organization, the Hellenic Club, existed for a time outside of DSO auspices. In 1972, it raised money to buy Christmas presents for a Greek orphanage. The club also organized a trip to Greece the following spring for fourteen boys and girls.

Following the merger, Malcolm Duffy and Rebecca Blackwell were instrumental in involving former ESB and Dwight students in community service, with the student body now beginning to see itself as one entity. From the late '70s into the early '80s, participation in community service was voluntary but encouraged by the guidance department. The suggested service involvement for seventh- through twelfth-graders was ten hours per week. Preliminary ideas for participation included Talk II (a peer counseling program), a campus tour guide program, and volunteering with local nursing homes, daycare facilities, and homeless shelters.

By 1982, visionary teachers and administrators Gene Wojtyla, Edie Lauderdale, Doris Gelman, and John Grundman joined Mr. Duffy and Ms. Blackwell in broadening and diversifying the community service experiences of the D-E students. Their work led to community service's becoming a graduation requirement. The goals of this requirement were formulated by a team of students and faculty: to develop a sense of community; to increase social awareness, initiative, responsibility, and compassion within the community; to give students a feeling of involvement in community problems and of

Seventh- and eighth-graders in April 1984 on a ten-mile walk-a-thon to benefit the Cerebral Palsy Foundation.

contributing to their solution; to understand one's culture through participation; and to improve school/community understanding.

The community service requirement took effect in 1986, mandating that students contribute a minimum of forty hours of service to a non-profit organization or persons in need. The program, according to Ms. Lauderdale, was "an opportunity to broaden your awareness of the world and the people around you." In tandem with this new requirement came a mandatory full-year ethics course, which evolved from a comparative religions/ethical behavior class.

"Education cannot be a valueless exercise," according to Dr. James Van Amburg. "It must focus on more than just academics. The character, integrity, and citizenship of our students are of critical concern to us. Our curriculum now provides a framework for teaching values and seeing them put into action in the community." Ms. Gelman was instrumental in guiding students during the early stages of the community service program. She worked with Nelson Chen and Alisa Gettenberg, both members of the Class of '86, on a community outreach program.

Doris Gelman (top) and Gene Wojtya (bottom) were among the strongest proponents of community service among D-E faculty.

The community service/ethics program included reflection after completion of service, which encouraged students to analyze and evaluate their participation and to make

Collecting goods for the food drive sponsored by CODES, Community Outreach of Dwight-Englewood School.

connections with ethical issues raised in their classes. "Values and ethics cannot be isolated from other aspects of the school experience," wrote Ms. Wojtyla, Upper School principal at the time. Though the community service/ethics program replaced the Dwight Service Organization, many individual clubs continued in the spirit and with the goals of DSO; in recent years these have included CODES (Community Outreach of DES), Action Against Homelessness, HOPE (Help Other People Everywhere), the Environmental Club, Makers of Tomorrow, and student government-sponsored community service activities.

The Class of 1988 was the first to complete the community service graduation requirement. Students volunteered at churches, hospitals, libraries, animal shelters, and with political organizations, accounting for 6,000 total hours of service. The program grew in scope and range under Mark Shultz, the ethics and community service coordinator in the '90s; in 1997, D-E students performed more than 9,200 hours of community service, testimony to the growth of the program over ten years. "Community service shows students their role in the greater world and teaches them how to live a life that is useful to others; in many cases, it opens a door and changes a student's world view," Upper School Principal Robert Brisk '76 said that year.

From 1986 to the present, Dwight-Englewood students have participated in such community service activities as working with young children at D-E's own Lower School and elsewhere, volunteering clerical services, assisting the physically challenged, volunteering at hospitals and health services,

Lower School students with Peter Davies, principal of the division, and the blankets collected for victims of Hurricane Sandy.

working at museums, getting involved in outdoor and conservation programs, working at assisted living facilities, volunteering with local government or political organizations, assisting in post-disaster cleanup (after, for instance, Superstorm Sandy), and working as first responders. (Ten years ago an article in the *Press Journal*, the local newspaper, reported that 10 percent of D-E seniors volunteered with an emergency service organization—as a first responder, EMT, or firefighter.) Since 1987, a Community Service Award has been given to a student who has shown service to the community well beyond the requirements.

For many students, in fact, the community service experience has meant much more than fulfilling a graduation requirement and has had a profound and life-changing effect.

"I now understand the problems of people who live in my community. I no longer have such

D-EFAC (D-E Fights Against Cancer) students play a "March Madness" fundraiser for cancer research.

"Dwight-Englewood has always instilled the importance of caring in the community." From *D-E Today*, 1997.

Students have constructed new or expanded existing gardens that serve not only as outdoor classrooms but also receive the outputs of our school's composting efforts AND provide delicious, organically grown ingredients for the dining halls.

a sheltered view," wrote Jeremy Dello Russo '93 in 1988. And this from Daniel Kaufman '88, recipient of both the D-E Community Service Award and the Rotary Club Award for Service: "It taught me many lessons about the world outside my own community. I am better able to understand some of the problems in the world and my own individual duty to help resolve those that I can. Most importantly, I have found my own voice, the courage to speak up in defense of something in which I believe."

Over the twenty-five years since the implementation of the community service/ethics graduation requirement, the Upper School in particular has been re-evaluating and fine-tuning the program to ensure its relevancy and value, but all three divisions are active in community service. The Thanksgiving food drive for the Englewood Center for Food Action is a school-wide project. There's the Lower School Community Garden, the Lower School toy drive for the Tomorrow Children's Fund at the Hackensack Medical Center, and the Lower School Jump Rope for Heart to raise funds for the American Heart Association. The Middle School Makers of Tomorrow Club has throughout the years sponsored many community service activities, such as providing backpacks filled with school supplies for children at Shelter Our Sisters and doing campus cleanup walks. Indeed, community service is an all-school commitment at Dwight-Englewood.

THE TECHNOLOGY REVOLUTION

Technology has long been a force at Dwight-Englewood School. From the first mainframe, housed in the former studio art room in Leggett Hall, computers played an increasingly important role in the academic program. The first formal technology-related academic course, labeled "Computer Mathematics" and a trimester in length, was offered in the year of the merger, under the aegis of the mathematics department. As the course description acknowledged, students brought vastly different levels of knowledge of the topic to the class, but the only opportunity for study beyond that one-trimester course lay in an extracurricular activity called the Computer Club. Before too long, that would change.

Technology of various sorts has been an important tool in the broader move to student-centered classrooms that takes into account the learning styles of individual students. The first mention of technology found in the archives of either school comes from the 1933 evaluation of the Englewood School for Boys by the Middle States Association of Schools and Colleges. Its description of the audio/visual program reads: "The school has its own moving picture projector and the use of another, together with a stereopticon. Moving pictures, lectures, and slides are presented in the gymnasium or in small groups in the classroom."

From that time on, archival documents show, teachers at both schools were aware that they should ask what each twentieth-century technological advance—recordings, moving pictures, radio, television, even film strips, slide projectors, and the Walkman—could and should add to the education of students.

In the late 1960s, Richard Zachary introduces ESB students to computer technology under the auspices of the mathematics department.

Opposite page: Chair of the French department Nicky Kovacs in the Dwight-Englewood language lab in Leggett Hall.

Peter Davies, here working with a Lower School student, was central in the school's development of a technology plan.

Even in the 1970s, D-E was attentive to teaching computer science and skills, but the technology has come a long way in the succeeding decades.

In 1993, with the support of the Upper School science and mathematics teachers, Assistant Headmaster Peter Davies was responsible for developing and implementing a technology plan for the school and was involved in creating (and eventually heading) the MST (integrated Math, Science, and Technology) program for grades nine through eleven. This involved reordering and realigning the curriculum so that what students were learning in science was reinforced by the mathematics they were studying. A technology course introduced students to computer programming, electronics, and other engineering topics and involved them in projects directly related to what they were studying in mathematics and science.

"Students should not only learn how to use existing technological tools but also understand how to create their own new tools to solve bigger and more interesting problems," Mr. Davies said at the time. "We don't want to use technologies just because they're new. We want to determine what makes sense for each department and grade level."

However, even in the mid-1990s, teachers across all grade levels and disciplines were still examining the role that audio/visual media should play in their bag of teaching tools. Some well-respected teachers at the time remained unsure of what and how extensive a role these new academic resources should play. By any estimate, however, their use had come a long way. At one end of the teaching spectrum were confident adopters who integrated recordings, slides, and filmed presentations smoothly and frequently into their classrooms. At the other end were those educators who, while recognizing that the availability of these media needed serious consideration, were wrestling with the question of how much centrality to give them.

Nevertheless, computer use among students was exploding. By 1995 there were sixty-five student computers for the Middle and Upper schools, all connected to the school's email system and the Internet. The Lower School had an additional thirty. "Labs are booked solid," Mr. Davies reported. "Teachers need to reserve space far in advance."

The mechanics of using AV materials would be an impediment right up to the end of the twentieth century. Only certain specialized classrooms were equipped with their own players and projection devices, and none had all the multiple types of hardware then available to choose from. On almost every occasion the teacher was required to order the appropriate machine in advance from the AV department; it had to be available at the specific time needed, and the teacher had to know how to run it successfully. The richness of the resources available was offset by the difficulty of accessing them.

By the early 2000s, the introduction of smaller machines with multiple uses —smartphones, tablet computers, and other hand-held devices—was presenting a technology challenge far greater than any faced before. Equally important, that challenge had to be met over a few short years rather than the century-long period over which technology for the classroom had previously evolved. Dwight-Englewood's response during the last years of Dr. Ralph Sloan's headship was swift. In October 2003, a news release announced the launching of the "Learning Unleashed Instructional Technology Initiative." Its main features included: wireless network access for students and faculty in all campus buildings; online course content through the Blackboard course management system; the "one-click classroom" initiative, which would eventually outfit every campus classroom with a projections device, VCR/DVD player, and control system; and a tablet PC provided to every teacher, which allowed them to quickly and effortlessly switch between computer and video/DVD presentations. Now a teacher was free to walk around the room while delivering notes on the screen from her pen-based computer.

Currently the D-E film course uses digital video and editing to teach students how to tell a story through short films. Students in Art History learn how presentation software can augment effective verbal skills. English classes find computers and projectors useful tools in group editing, and history classes explore the impact of blogging on the way our society communicates and uses information.

Lionel Garrison (at left, with a group of math stalwarts in 1979) was instrumental in the school's early work with computers. With the opening of the new athletic center in 1978, the old Dwight gym became home of the mathematics department.

By 2007, the backpacks of all students in grades six through twelve would include, along with their pens and notebooks, a tablet PC to use both at home and at school. The tablet PC pilot program began in the fall of 2004 under the direction of the technology department's Trevor Shaw. Sixth-grade teachers Jacklyn Tchang, who joined the faculty in 2001, and Joan Sommer, a long-tenured teacher who came to Dwight-Englewood with the

iPads and tablet PCs are ubiquitous tools for learning at D-E today.

Bede merger, were the first to integrate tablet technology into their math and science classrooms. According to Joan Sommer, "Both Jakke Tchang and I both realized that introducing tablets was a milestone for the school. We had this opportunity to develop interactive, thought-provoking experiences that made our students more engaged and active learners. Lessons that we developed using tablet technology allowed us to observe the thinking processes of our students. For example, we witnessed how they thought when they were using the tablets to teach fellow students their strategy for solving a math problem or to analyze downloaded data from a weather website about hurricanes. Right from the start, the students embraced the tablet PCs with enthusiasm and made their personal computers a tool for their own personal approach to learning."

The success of the sixth-grade pilot program demonstrated that tablet PC technology could play an effective role in education, and the practice soon spread to the entire Middle and Upper schools within the next three years. At the same time of this "technology surge" in the Middle and Upper schools, multiple rolling carts of tablet PCs began providing Lower School students access in any classroom to individual computers whenever their teacher needed them for instruction.

Though the problem of easy access to all types of technology thus had been solved, the challenge of learning how to employ that technology in a sound educational program remained ahead. In 2003, Trevor Shaw, D-E's director of academic technology during the development of the tablet PC initiative, summarized the school's overall philosophy on the use of technology.

"Dwight-Englewood has always put instructional objectives first," he wrote, "and allowed curriculum to drive the implementation of hardware and software." This succinctly summarized the past history of not only the school's use of technology in instruction but also its broader changes in pedagogy. At the same time, it is a wise roadmap for the wholly necessary but potentially rocky road ahead. More recently, the introduction of a new iPad curriculum in the Middle School in 2014 was the first step in what will be a school-wide initiative.

The current physical cornerstone of Dwight-Englewood's technology focus is the Taub Technology Center, which opened in November 2007 in the space in the Imperatore Library formerly occupied by the school's Bookstore and Coop, which had been relocated the previous year to the Klein Campus Center. The Taub Center contains a 640-square-foot computer lab, plus an office and workshop space for the computer services department. Semicircular in shape and equipped with the most up-to-date technology, the main room is an attractive venue for small meetings and lectures.

The Taub Center was "a huge step forward," according to Mr. Shaw. "It's great to now have the team responsible for maintaining D-E's technology in a single location," he said at the time of the opening. "Problems get solved more quickly when all of your resources are at arm's length." Attractive and comfortable, the Taub Center welcomes students and faculty alike throughout the day to use the computers. Perhaps even more important, it's where they can go to resolve any computer-related problems they encounter. In addition to computers, the center is equipped with the standard "one-click" audio/visual set-up, with a ceiling-mounted LCD projector, DVD players, and the ability to project wirelessly from a tablet computer.

With these and other tools, faculty today continue their quest to identify sound educational practice regarding technology as they implement the rapid and dramatic changes in curriculum and pedagogy that unquestionably will define Dwight-Englewood's educational program in the years following its celebration of the 125 years since Dwight School's founding.

HOW WE LIVED AND WHAT WE REMEMBER

While what goes on in the classrooms and laboratories and studios and gymnasiums, and on the stages and the playing fields, defines the enduring essence of Dwight-Englewood School, alumni through the decades also remember fondly the non-academic and non-athletic side of their lives on campus: what they did and what they valued. These memories can be potent indeed, and traditions recalled are often fraught with emotion.

Traditions ran especially deep at Dwight; memories of them survive with clarity, and for many girls, music runs through them. "A more gentlemanly gentleman you'll never meet," Eve LeBan Drew '64 has written of Joseph Erwin. She sang for him in Choir and Choral Club and was president of Bell Choir. "Those bells were crafted by angels, I'm sure." But popular music left its mark too. "Before its release," she said, "I heard my good friend and classmate Leslie Gore's 'It's My Party' in Mr. Erwin's music room. She became a star overnight and rivaled The Beatles in popularity."

Though Dwight did have an alma mater, the song that most stirs alumnae emotions is "Jerusalem," the poem by William Blake (not his title for it) that Sir Charles Hubert Hastings Perry set to music and which begins, "And did these feet in ancient times...." For four decades this was sung, with words slightly altered, as the processional at graduation ceremonies, and since all upper-class students were required to attend graduation ceremonies, by the time they themselves were seniors "Jerusalem" was special to them. ESB did have a routinely sung alma mater, "Veritas Fortissima." ("Fortissima Veritas," meaning "Truth is Strongest" in Latin, was the school's motto, "graven on our shield," as the song had it. The Dwight motto was "Per ardua, astra," which translates as, "Through struggles or adversity, the stars." The D-E motto, "Per ardua, ad veritatem," or "Through hard work, we arrive at the truth," gives a nod to both.) In recalling their years at Dwight School, older alumnae remember that a DWIGHT girl was thought to be: **D**ependable, **W**illing, **I**ndustrious, **G**racious, **H**onorable, and **T**houghtful. Today Dwight-Englewood incorporates the school's current motto "Challenging Minds for a Changing World" to all aspects of the school experience.

"Jerusalem" was a sectarian hymn, of course, which suggests another core characteristic of the schools, Dwight especially, virtually up to the 1973 merger.

"I felt that I was in a school with Presbyterian roots," recalls Theresa Filippi Loverro '59. "Graduation was held at the First Presbyterian Church and 'Jerusalem' was central to the ceremony. We heard and sang more hymns in chapel services at the start of each day." A two-semester Bible course was a requirement, but Jewish girls were excused from the second semester, which covered the New Testament.

And though there was less religious observance at the Boys' School, its early ties with "First Pres" were tight (in fact, essential to the school's survival), and long-serving headmaster Marshall Umpleby recalled years later that he had been called on the carpet by his board chair for accepting a boy who might have been Jewish; the same chair took a "sneering attitude" to families from such places as Teaneck and Hackensack, "anything west of Engle Street being beyond the pale," Mr. Umpleby recalled. In those days, most students came from Englewood or Tenafly. Eventually that would change, of course, and dramatically.

The Christmas Pageant, a series of tableaux depicting Nativity scenes from the Old Masters, with narration and with the Bell Choir and Choral Club performing, was the highlight of the season at Dwight. To be chosen as Madonna (the faculty made the selection, based on citizenship) was a great honor, and portraits of all the Madonnas hung in senior study. The narrator was a coveted role as well. Along with the Pageant (today there is a holiday concert), other Christmas traditions have come and gone: a luncheon for seniors and college-age alumnae home for the holidays and caroling by seniors the night before school closed for Christmas, with a pajama party afterwards.

This is the 1968 version of the Christmas Pageant, a long-standing Dwight tradition.

Opposite page: In 1925, founding co-principal Euphemia S. Creighton's car, her driver, Laurie, her dog, and boarders.

Some traditions, of course, were wholly secular. There was Field Day, with competition between white and yellow teams. Seniors took care of their "sister class," the sophomores, with each senior looking after a "little sister." Teddy bear Geoffrey Chaucer as the mascot of the senior class is among the most cherished and long-lived traditions; from 1904 Geoffrey (named for the poet Geoffrey Chaucer) was handed down to each succeeding senior class into the 1960s.

Senior class mascot Geoffrey Bear.

In 1911, boarders in The Cottage had a slumber party of the roof.

The Father-Daughter Dance was memorable, and joint Dwight-Boys' School dances were among the few occasions when the twain would meet. Graduates speak of a "Mason-Dixon Line" between the schools, adjacent since ESB's move to 363 East Palisade Avenue in 1937.

"Our sports field was next to the boys' sports field," Ms. Loverro wrote. "When afternoon classes on the east side of Leggett Hall got boring, especially in warm weather, we could look out and see the boys playing baseball." Stefan Bucek '75 also recalls the separation.

"In Form II, as we called eighth grade, I took a typing class in Leggett Hall.... I was actually scared to walk over there, lest I might run into one of the girls I'd know and might have to talk to her. So, initially, my interactions with the opposite gender were somewhat strained."

"Christmas Dance to be Given," ran the headline in the December 1937 *Spectator*, the Englewood School newspaper. "A dance shall be given the 20th of December, 1937, in the school gymnasium," said the article, "and shall be controlled and regulated by a Senior Committee.... Although the first idea was to give a 'Football' dance for increasing the athletic funds, as the likelihood of making any money seemed very small, the committee changed its plans and is putting on a dance completely separate from the football organization." The entrance fee was $1.50, "per couple or 'stag'," and the dance was scheduled to run from nine o'clock to one.

"Many girls attended Miss Florence's Fortnightly Dance Classes at the Englewood Field Club," Melinda Ruth Swango Johnson '55 recalled. This was a white-glove affair, but Field Club membership wasn't required to attend. "Most of my friends hated it," wrote Susan Devine-Lempert '74, "but I loved learning how to do the Lindy Hop, a social skill that has come in handy over the years."

Many Dwight traditions surrounded graduation, where seniors wore white dresses (in some eras identical, chosen by a committee) and carried yellow roses. At a Class Day banquet, juniors received their school rings and the Alumnae Association presented each senior with a gift. The school head and the seniors chose junior girls to carry the "Smilax Chain" of greens at graduation.

The junior class president served as marshal and carried a basket with the diplomas. A baccalaureate service for seniors was meditative in nature.

"We had moving-up day," Ms. Loverro remembered, "when we composed and sang songs to the seniors, sang the 'banner song' as incoming seniors received a big felt banner. We retired the banner song, I think, in my senior year. Mrs. Bailey said it was passé." Thus would many traditions languish and die, out of step with the evolving times. The counterculture '60s were particularly hard on them, as students and faculty alike marched to a different drummer.

"Gone was the simplicity and naiveté of the 1950s," recalled Ms. Johnson, who was president

The Smilax Chain.

The graduating Class of 1938.

of the Dwight Alumnae Association at the time of the merger and teamed up with the ESB alumni president to draft new bylaws for the combined association, which she then headed. In 1953, a student poll at Dwight selected *I Love Lucy* as its favorite TV program, and Doris Day and Eddie Fisher were chosen as favorite singers. In 1956, Dwight's question of the month was, "Do you think seniors should be allowed to wear lipstick at school?" A different world was not far ahead.

Over the years, there have been various restrictions on and conventions of dress at both schools.

"Dwight day students never wore uniforms except for an 'experimental' program from 1966 to 1972," according to Vici LaSala '42. Otherwise the dress code had been "consistent: skirts, blouses, sweaters over a blouse, cardigan sweaters, jackets or blazers, socks or stockings, and shoes (no sneakers)." The uniform varied but "included kilts or A-line skirts, white blouses, cardigans or blazers, knee socks and shoes."

"Of course the skirts were supposed to touch our knees," Ms. Devine-Lempert remembers, "but as the sixties progressed into the seventies we all rolled up the waists so we looked like a bunch of knobby-kneed girls with extremely thick middles."

At ESB, ties and jackets or blazers, no sneakers, were the norm for decades, up until the last pre-merger years.

"I kind of enjoyed putting on a blazer and tie each day," Mr. Bucek recalled. "Frankly, I was sort of sorry to see it go." He no doubt was in the minority, as most students on both sides of the so-called "Mason-Dixon Line" reveled in their newfound freedoms, which involved much more than dress. Jeans, t-shirts, and sneakers were still not allowed; collared shirts and corduroys or non-denim pants became the customary attire for boys and skirts, dresses, or long pants other than jeans for girls. At first, Tuesday remained "dress-up day," when girls were required to wear skirts or dresses and boys ties and jackets for assemblies. By the mid-1980s, all this had changed again and jeans, t-shirts, and sneakers had become acceptable; although a dress code of sorts remained, it was both loose and loosely enforced. Per the student manual, clothing should be neat, clean, and modest and not be too short, tight, revealing, or tattered.

The voice of the student body has always been amplified through some form of representation at the schools. Student government at Dwight had its start in 1900 when the girls volunteered to regulate themselves in certain school activities. This was successful, so the school went on to form an honor system as its form of government, and later the students had written a constitution, which provided that members of student council, or senate, "were chosen each semester by and for the student body and designed to create a spirit of friendliness and cooperation between students and faculty."

The Englewood School for Boys had adopted a traditional system of representation, with three boys elected from each of the five highest forms as a student council to tackle the pressing issues of the day. Then, in 1950, an honor board was established as part of the council to "curb the serious epidemic of unauthorized collaboration on not only homework but on quizzes and examinations. The board has jurisdiction over all cases involving cheating, theft, or destruction of property."

The first student government of the Dwight-Englewood School was formed in 1974. In 1976, the D-E newsletter reported that its "main goal is to improve communication so that more school spirit and unity can be achieved." By the late '70s, it was considered the single most important student activity on campus.

Throughout the twentieth century, wars created, defined, and shaped epochs, and this is reflected in the microcosmic history of our schools as much as in society in general, and no war was more devastating and all-embracing than World War II. With its virtually all-male population, the Englewood School for Boys was naturally even more devastatingly affected by the war than Dwight School, though of course Dwight families felt the impact too, and many Dwight alumnae were involved in war work of some sort.

Founded in 1928, roughly a decade after World War I ended, ESB was barely a teenager when Pearl Harbor was attacked, sending the United States into war. The school was just beginning to recover from the near-knockout punches of the Depression. Some 70 percent of the Englewood School faculty would go to war. Assistant Headmaster E. Butler Beaumont became Captain Beaumont in the Army Air Force; Senior Master Albert L. Metzger became First Lieutenant Metzger, also in the Army Air Force; and Luke Ward, who led the school's athletic program, became Staff Sergeant James L. Ward in the Army.

Marshall Umpleby, who carried on as headmaster, wrote a letter to alumni on January 1, 1945. "Greetings from ESB," it opened. "Wherever you are we are still thinking of you, and we wonder how you are faring in this fourth winter of the war.... The Englewood School, still known locally as the Boys' School, seems to bear up," he reported, with 110 students enrolled. "More science and less Latin, perhaps, but we are still cluttered with languages.... We have resumed interscholastic games after a lay-off of four years. The idea was to save traveling."

"Gasoline rationing precluded travel beyond a five-mile radius," he recalled years later. "Instead of trips to Newark, Elizabeth, Plainfield, and New York, the football and baseball teams played the second teams of the public high schools in Englewood, Leonia, Tenafly, and Teaneck. Basketball was entirely intramural."

Two of the three PT Boat captains—Lieutenant Robert Searles '36 (left) and Lieutenant Leonard Nikoloric '35 (center)—pictured on this *LIFE* cover were ESB graduates (and Princeton alumni).

The Alumni House garage was moved next to the "demountable" building, then the gym, to serve as a field house and was dedicated in 1948 to the eight Boys' School alumni who died in the war.

ESB students doing calisthenics as part of World War II preparedness.

departments of the school. His talk was of a serious nature and concerned our part in the war effort. He stressed the importance of building ourselves up both physically and mentally to meet the challenge with which we are faced."

A school, like the proverbial army, travels on its stomach, and *The Spectator*, in an April 1943 issue, naturally covered the impact of food rationing at ESB.

"Recently fresh meat, fats (butter, Crisco, etc.) and canned fish have gone on the rationed list," the editors reported. "This means that whereas we had meat four times a week last year, we now can expect it but twice."

Englewood School faculty served in the Korean War as well, though that conflict didn't decimate the teaching core as World War II had, and the Vietnam War caused no faculty attrition, yet that conflict, and the social revolution that embraced it, had a huge effect on the schools.

The most somber news in Mr. Umpleby's New Year's letter was that there were five "Gold Stars" among the 206 stars in the ESB service flag—five casualties among the 206 alumni (from 289 alumni of record) known to be serving. The first, *The Spectator* reported in a headline, had been Paul B. Santee '38, when his airplane crashed in January 1943.

After the United States entered the war, ESB had embraced the obligation of preparing its students for leadership in the military.

"Beginning in the spring of 1942," Bruce LaSala '47 recalled decades later, "the school instituted a training program in which everyone, seventh-graders on up, would fall out in formation in close-order drill. Like the rest of the country, the school was galvanized by the war effort. The atmosphere was that of a military school."

"Headmaster Considers Service Demands Urgent," bannered an April 1942 issue of *The Spectator*. "During the Activities Period on Wednesday, April 1," the story read, "Mr. Umpleby addressed the assembled Intermediate and Senior

Dwight had its Father-Daughter Dinner and Englewood School its Father-Son version, shown here in 1946.

The Rifle Club was a popular activity at ESB for many years. With advisor Richard Overton, the members are about to enter the range under the old gymnasium in the Korean War year of 1953.

Dwight boarders in the common room of The Cottage in 1941. In 1955, the boarding program would be phased out.

"Flower Power was beginning to get a foothold in the country's soul," Paul Sammarco '66 wrote, recalling the tumultuous '60s, "and a whole new generation was grasping at it like a life-saver in rough seas. The Vietnam War was escalating and receiving bad press. Many feared the draft. We experienced Kennedy's assassination, which was horrid and frightening for our generation but which the school handled very well—particularly Mr. Metzger, who kept his chin up at all times."

In 1970, a Dwight student reported attending a January 28 Moratorium Concert at Madison Square Garden. "There were long-haired straights, a few Hare Krishnas, maybe," she said, "but what really surprised me the most was when I found none other than [Dwight English teacher] Mrs. Sagan sitting in the second row."

In the 1970s, both Dwight and Englewood School for Boys students participated in the American Field Service, which was most active in the 1980s under the leadership of Johanna Gambrill, a D-E parent and later faculty member. She had been an AFS participant herself and was passionate about the organization's philosophy.

"The purpose of AFS," she felt, "was to broaden a young person's view of the world beyond one's cultural comfort zone. By living with a family in another country, an individual can find a common humanity. The goal of AFS was to change the attitudes of young people towards those of diverse cultures" so they could "be leaders of change back in their own communities. Students from around the world would work to fulfill the motto of AFS which comes from the Sanskrit language: 'Walk together, talk together, O ye peoples of the earth; for then and only then shall ye have peace." American Field Service was phased out at D-E in the early '90s, but it led to the formation of other cultural exchange programs.

By then the language department had been considering introducing a non-Western language in the Upper School. Japanese was chosen because of the support from the many local Japanese families. Also, there was a robust culture attached to the language. The exchange began with a letter and then a visit in the spring of 1990 from school administrators from

The Dwight-Englewood cheerleading squad in 1981. Brooke Shields '83 is in the center of the group.

Okayama, Japan. That summer, Bill Buckmiller, director of the business office; Jane White, the language department chair; and Janet Glass, a Spanish teacher with personal contacts in Japan, went to observe a number of Japanese schools in order to establish a "sister school" relationship, which would enhance the new Japanese language program.

Starting in 1991, five or six Japanese students came here for home-stays of two weeks. Each lived with a D-E family and attended school. In return, an equal number of D-E students went to stay with families in Okayama. Japanese language classes were offered from 1990 through 2000, and the Japanese Exchange Program continued another ten years as a cultural exchange.

A favorite off-campus haunt of generations of Dwighties and Boys' School students, Baumgart's Café in downtown Englewood, was a regular advertiser in *The Spectator*, and its ads were typically larger than those of the other downtown Englewood businesses. One in April 1942 for the "Tasty, Wholesome Luncheonette" offered "Extra flavor, pure, fresh-from-freezer Ice Cream." Today Baumgart's is in part unchanged, with its classic sign, soda fountain, and homemade ice cream. But just as Chinese cuisine is now a Baumgart's staple along with the ice cream sodas of yesteryear, so has the way Dwight-Englewood students act, dress, and think about the world shifted dramatically, most often mirroring the broader society. D-E's move to diversity—ethnically, racially, and culturally—has been nothing short of remarkable, and now clearly defines the school.

"We really broadcast quite loudly that this is a diverse place," Peter Davies, then the D-E director of admissions, told a *New York Times* reporter in October 1991, and it's only gotten more so since then. "It's so diverse, I don't think any one group can say they're in the majority." The reporter said Dwight-Englewood "is often cited as a model multicultural school."

Today's Dwight-Englewood is in fact the most ethnically diverse secondary school in Bergen County, with a student and faculty body representing more than seventy-five languages spoken at home in addition to English. The school's Diversity Values Statement, authored by a committee of faculty and administrators and officially introduced by the Office of MultiCultural Affairs in 2014, speaks to the valuing of this reality.

Students from these most recent decades at D-E will no doubt remember their own traditions after they graduate, but among them will inevitably be the demands of rigorous studies.

"The only tradition I remember from my ESB days," Mr. Sammarco reported of his experience nearly half a century ago, "was going to Baumgart's for a cheeseburger and a Cherry Coke after a long day of being buried in academic information."

Asked to name the fundamental values that were part of Dwight when she was a student, Toddy Naiswald Powers '38 was clear: "Remember who you are and what you represent!"

The Cultural Diversity Club in 1991.

Dwight-Englewood's greatest asset is alumni who come back to campus every year during Reunion/Commencement Weekend.

WHAT'S PAST IS PROLOGUE

Dear Friends:

This 2013–2014 year at Dwight-Englewood School has honored the traditions of our past, recognized present-day innovations, and challenged us to envision bright possibilities for the future. The pages of this book have come together also to sincerely thank those who have contributed in myriad ways to our success and enduring value.

This is a unique moment in the life of Dwight-Englewood, and it is also the best of times to be involved in schools. With emerging research on teaching and learning, combined with the most current brain research and new developments in technology, an exciting renaissance in education is underway. This is an era of greater understanding about teaching and learning. As an independent school, Dwight-Englewood has the freedom to explore and then incorporate the most exceptional findings and best practices from around the world into our ever-improving, growing program.

The Dwight-Englewood student body spells out the celebratory number on Leggett Field.

A preview of the STEM (Science, Technology, Engineering, and Mathematics) building, to be located adjacent to Leggett Hall.

The Robotics Center in the STEM building.

In the summer of 2014, we will begin to build our new STEM (Science, Technology, Engineering, and Mathematics) building, which will be located adjacent to Leggett Hall—the oldest academic building on our campus. The program development and design stages for this new facility have already begun to shape our program in new ways. STEM represents the best of what Dwight-Englewood School has offered in education, and what we can become. While we can't predict exactly what will result from our ongoing efforts, we understand that we must educate our children for their futures, not our past. We are driven by the pace and paths set by our predecessors. And, like those who came before us, we are engaged in consistent, passionate mindfulness to updating curriculum, offering new courses, implementing new pedagogies, and coming to know well new generations of students.

Finally and most importantly, we are consistently cognizant of the obligations that accompany the significant privileges associated with being a part of Dwight-Englewood School. There are infinite possibilities here, due to individuals' ideas, productive collaborations, and the wide range of resources available. Our Mission Statement speaks to this inherent responsibility and could not be more appropriate for the times in which we live: "We seek excellence, honor integrity, and embrace diversity in order to develop the skills, values, and courage to meet the challenges of a changing world and make it better."

Thank you for being a part of our exceptional "community of learners."

Warmly,
Dr. Rodney V. De Jarnett
Head of School